T0307048

Throw Away
Your Loincloth

Throw Away Your Loincloth

Michelle Jones

BOOKS

Winchester, UK
Washington, USA

First published by O-Books, 2014
O-Books is an imprint of John Hunt Publishing Ltd., Laurel House, Station Approach,
Alresford, Hants, SO24 9JH, UK
office1@jhpbooks.net
www.johnhuntpublishing.com

For distributor details and how to order please visit the 'Ordering' section on our website.

Text copyright: Michelle Jones 2013

ISBN: 978 1 78099 115 3

A CIP catalogue record for this book is available from the British Library.

Design: Lee Nash

Printed in the USA by Edwards Brothers Malloy

We operate a distinctive and ethical publishing philosophy in all
areas of our business, from our global network of authors to
production and worldwide distribution.

CONTENTS

Preface

I have spent most of my adult life rushed off my feet, or collapsed in a sticky exhausted heap. From chasing a career to chasing after the kids, it's been hectic. Finding time for myself has always been a challenge, but I still want to have something for me – and while I'm at it, I'd quite like to feel happy and content, achieve my dreams, and believe in magic. If you can identify with this, then this book is for you, with my love.

Chapter 1

Is This You?

Wakey Wakey! The alarm clock sounds and you really don't want to drag yourself out of bed. Another day of hurtling around from home to work, childminder's to school, meeting to meeting. If you are at home with young children you may feel lucky if you manage to get dressed, let alone leave the house at some point. Another day feeling that life is somehow passing you by...

I was in that place for years. The situations may change from day to day, but the feeling is the same. I'm not saying that I was unhappy in those years, but I needed something more, something that said 'This is me'.

To be frank, "I want it all, and I want it now"... words of wisdom sung by the very wonderful rock band Queen; a tongue-in-cheek tribute to our culture – but you know what? It's true, I do want it all, and yes, I most definitely want it now. I want to follow my heart, achieve my dreams, not have to worry about money... I don't mind having to work for it, although it would be nice if it didn't take too much time out of my day; I want to feel connected to nature, to the greater world, to God – whatever or whoever that might be, but I can't be doing with all that sitting around meditating – after all, even if I did possess a loincloth, I certainly would not have the time (or energy) to sit around contemplating my navel for hours (I wouldn't be able to get up again either), while sat on top of a mountain in Tibet! (Deep breath.)

In any case, a loincloth is hardly flattering!

Do you feel the same?

It's natural to have dreams, to want a better life for yourself and your loved ones. It's also completely reasonable to want to feel happy and content, but achieving this can be a challenge. I believe that the key to success – in all areas of life – lies in how we deal with the stuff in our head and our heart, from the little everyday dramas and irritations, to the major events that can change our course and shape our future. I've had experience of a few of those myself, and I'll tell you all about them later. And then there's the 'Spiritual Life', the deep and meaningful inner connections...

We are told that if we live a spiritual life, we are better equipped to be happier, healthier, more successful, wealthier people. We find it easier to pursue – and achieve – our dreams, whatever those dreams might be... but what do we mean by living a 'spiritual life'?

It's a big question, and a tricky one to answer. For some, it means following a specific faith or religion – but I am talking about a different kind of 'spiritual life', one that you can integrate with your faith, or follow on its own. There are many people who don't subscribe to an organized religion, but who still want to live that 'spiritual life'. How those people tap into the spiritual, that sense of connection to the 'something' that is just out of reach of our physical senses is a deeply personal thing. If you do follow a particular faith, I hope that you will still find inspiration here; I do not believe that there is any 'right' or 'wrong' answer. I certainly cannot believe that when we eventually shake off our mortal bodies, our souls ascend to some form of compartmentalized heaven where the Christians sit in one corner, the Buddhists in another, and so on. If that were the case, then even in those corners there would be different factions – within Christianity there are who knows how many subdivisions... Catholics, Protestants, Methodists, Wesleyans, Quakers, Mormons... need I go on? I can see it now, like a vast burger restaurant in the sky filled with different children's parties: "You're here with the Greek Gods? They're over there next to the Mount Olympus bouncy castle..."

A wise man once said that:

There are many paths up the mountain, but they all lead to the same summit.

That is how I think of the variety and diversity of different religions; each is a different path, but each reaches the same summit. If we took that divided heaven argument to its logical conclusion, then I think heaven would be exactly the same as earth... full of squabbling people who each think that their way is 'right'!

This book does not claim to be 'right' in any way, shape or form. It is just one path, one woman's opinion, my way of making sense of the world and living within it in a way that gives me hope and inspiration.

Throughout these pages, I am going to have to refer to the 'something' that we might think of as a deity. You may call him/her/it by different names, but I am not going to tie myself up in knots trying to be politically correct and nondenominational. I am just going to say God. It makes it simple and I can type the word easily without a fuss. This does not mean I do not believe in the existence of a Goddess, or any other part of the holy family, it is just easier, the name of the god/gods/goddesses I pray to is irrelevant and I have no desire to influence your choice of deity. You can substitute God for whichever word you can relate to, I won't be offended!

So now we've got that out of the way, let's go back to the original question:

What do we mean by 'Living a spiritual life'?

My spiritual life means that I want to feel a connection to everything; I want there to be a God and angels to guard me and guide me, an afterlife to look forward to and an energy in everything around me that I can sense, from animals and plants to the stars and planets – including our own earth. Do you think I want

I don't think so. I have been working on building
nections since I was a child, and I have seen and heard
n, personally experienced too much, for me to believe
se.

me give you an example.

you believe you have a Guardian Angel; someone
ling out for you wherever you are, whatever you do? I
ve you do, in fact I know you do; but as you need to build on
tionships with your friends, so you need to build on your
ationship with your Guardian Angel too. If you don't call your
st friend regularly, he or she might wonder what they have
one to offend you; if you ignore them for a long time, they might
assume that you no longer want them as a friend at all! The good
news is that you cannot do anything that will make your angel
turn his back on you, but you can certainly build a closer
relationship so that when you really need his help, he is there like
a shot.

A couple of years ago, we went off on one of our regular trips
to Finland. My husband Phil worked out there some years ago
and we absolutely love the country, so we go off as often as we
can. This was one of our January shopping trips to the sales in
Helsinki and we were really looking forward to it. However, a
couple of days before we flew out, I had a little accident.

It was one of those stupid moments that you can see yourself
doing – but are completely powerless to stop... I was walking
around indoors with nothing on my feet; Phil was sat in his usual
place watching the TV, and as I passed him to get to the sofa, I
caught his booted foot with my toes. It was agonizing, I could not
put my foot flat on the floor and moving the toe next to my big
toe was just excruciating. I know now that I had actually broken
the toe, but at the time I could not see the point in going to the
local Accident and Emergency department and waiting for hours
only to be told I had broken my toe and there was nothing they
could do about it...

So I just did what any woman would do in the circumstances. I blamed Phil. He should not have had his foot sticking out. Completely unjust of course (you see, dear, I am apologizing!) but I needed someone to blame to make me feel better. The toe began to turn black… and it became tricky to get my boots on, but nonetheless we were going off for our holiday.

On the morning of the flight, I squeezed my foot into my boot and hobbled into the car. I managed to avoid running my feet over with the case and we checked in the baggage without incident.

When our flight was called, we went to the departure gate and sat down with the other passengers; there were a lot of them. Phil needed to use the loo, so off he went – and while he was gone, they called for all the passengers to board a bus to take us to the plane. I had to wait for Phil to come back of course, and so I sat there and watched as everyone else crammed into the bus. As the passengers boarded, I was asking my Guardian Angel for a bit of help here; please please please, don't let my bad toe be trodden on… but I could not see how on earth I could avoid it, or how my Guardian Angel could possibly help! I was utterly convinced that I was in for a lot of pain; the bus was completely packed, standing room only, not only with people but with all their hand luggage squashed in on the floor as well.

Phil returned and helped me to hobble over to the waiting bus; the double doors halfway down the side were open and I stared in at the solid mass of bodies. A sea of faces stared back; I didn't see how we were going to get on at all, let alone manage it without my poor foot getting seriously trodden on!

At this point my Guardian Angel earned his money; the bus driver appeared out of nowhere and looked us in the eyes – "Come on," he said, "there's a couple of seats at the front." Seats? How on earth were there any actual seats left on the bus! Somehow, there were; two glorious seats, right behind the bus driver, miraculously unoccupied. I felt the burning gaze of the other passengers as we boarded through the front doors and sat down...

The driver got on, started the engine and drove across the tarmac towards our waiting Finnair plane. My next concern was the inevitable crush in the aisle of the plane – you know how it goes, everyone trying to put their hand luggage up in the overhead lockers, while the other passengers attempt to push past them... it's a recipe for disaster when you have a broken toe.

My Guardian Angel was there again, right on cue. The bus stopped, the driver did not open the doors in the middle of the bus at all... he opened the doors at the front and refused to let anyone else disembark before we did... I was the very first person up the steps to the plane, the first person inside the plane, the first person to take their seat – and mine was by the window, so I didn't even have to move to let anyone else in!

Now I don't care what you think – there is absolutely no way on this blessed earth that was ever going to happen on its own. I know that it only happened because my Guardian Angel arranged it for me. Thank you thank you thank you...

That is just one example of the countless times that my Guardian Angel has been there for me – and the really good news is that your Guardian Angel is just waiting to help you too... there is a lot more on this subject in a later chapter.

Of course, living a spiritual life is not just about sitting around and waiting for your Guardian Angel to do all the work for you. We have to make an effort to actually work on our connections and senses...

... And that's where the main issue (for me at any rate) comes in.

Time.

I don't know about you, but my life seems to be completely hectic! The days pass by so fast I don't know where they are going, and I never seem to have any time for me... I know that I'm not on my own with this, my friends, my family – in fact everyone tells me they have exactly the same issues. Most of us have to work (congratulations if you are one of the lucky ones of independent means!) to live, and then there are the demands of our families, maintaining our homes, enjoying a social life and all the little daily things that only take moments, but which build up into large chunks of time over a period.

If you added up all the time spent on the routine 'it'll only take 2 minutes' chores, how much time every week would you spend opening the post, emptying the bin, wiping down the draining board and work surfaces, cleaning your teeth, putting the washing in the washing machine (the washing appears a lot in this book, it's an occupational hazard for mums)... and taking it out again, hanging it up, plumping cushions, making the bed... If you have young children, you'll be lucky to get 15 minutes to yourself every day, especially if you go out to work as well! I was on the work/childminder/school run treadmill for quite a few years and it's exhausting. You have my sympathies, but the good news is that it does not last forever, children grow up – and if you train them right, they'll do some of the routine chores for you! We have only partially succeeded in this.

All the technology we have nowadays doesn't seem to make things any easier either; it's just another layer of stuff to distract you. Checking e-mails on your phone, playing daft games with your friends, sending text messages instead of calling people... and of course, Facebook and Twitter. Social networking may bring the world to your mobile device, but it also keeps you away from the world; the real world that is. I use it myself, but I have it under control these days; I had a phase of not sleeping well, which I believe was down to staring at a screen for too long every evening. (This very issue has been on the news this week, it seems I am right!) It is an area of concern for me, that our young people all seem to have busy social lives... through a set of headphones and a screen with an avatar. You don't need to be a psychologist to see that we are storing up trouble for the future unless something happens to change this. There is no substitute for face to face relationships and some fresh air!

I have to tell you this: one of my sons went to a party recently; he is a huge fan of online gaming and seems to have the enviable (?) ability to manage several screens and a conversation simultaneously. Anyway, he went to a party with real people, in a real place... and was completely wiped out the following day. I asked him why he was so tired, after all, he had gone to bed hours earlier than he does when he's gaming – and he replied that it was "exhausting talking to real people!" This is going to be a huge social issue if we don't tackle it soon; where does it lead? Sorry, I'm digressing, but it is an issue which is not going to go away.

With all this going on, how on earth do you find time to work on your spiritual well-being? Is there any point in worrying about it anyway! I believe that there is, because if you feed your soul, the rest of your life seems to fall into place.

Throughout this book, I am going to show you how you can integrate your spiritual self into every corner of your life, how it can enable you to feel happier, become more productive, more successful, and how to feel at peace. Oh yes, feeling at peace – just about the best feeling in the world. I can manage this about 40% of the time now. I suspect that the ratio of 'feeling at peace' to either 'rushing around like a crazed loon' to 'actively worrying over something' is really low for most people, most of the time. I will talk about this in a later chapter, bear with me.

The good news is that you don't need to find any 'extra' time in order to achieve this spiritual life. I have never had time to sit still, so I have always carried my spiritual life with me, taking the opportunities to 'plug in' wherever and whenever I can. I'm still learning. I don't believe you ever stop learning, although if I did actually pack my mythical loincloth and shimmy on up to the mountain for a spot of deep navel contemplation, I could probably manage to become serene just before the universe finally collapses in on itself. Or not.

I have two other jobs as well as being a writer and author. I enjoy both of them and would find it difficult to give them up, even if I were to become 'rich and famous'! I work in the market town of Petersfield in the South Downs National Park; there is no public transport that gets me where I need to be at the right time, so I drive the ten miles up the A3 and park in a little lane just outside the center. It takes me about ten minutes to walk from my car into work, across a very busy road and then down a stunningly beautiful path. I had been travelling back and forth from Petersfield for more than 20 years on a regular basis and had never once noticed this path. It is right in the center of town, alongside an incredibly busy road, and yet somehow it manages to be serene and peaceful. There are trees of oak, ash, hornbeam, beech and hazel overhanging a green passage with a clear running stream to one side, and depending on the time of year, there are a wide variety of plants, from cow parsley and daffodils, to blackberries, bluebells and daisies. The noise of the traffic seems far away, drowned out by the sound of the birds singing their little hearts out. I love it; the colors change with the seasons, fresh pale greens and creams in the spring, richer greens in the summer, then golden russets in the autumn giving way to grey bare branches and glossy dark holly leaves in winter.

Even though I am right in the center of town, there is an otherworldliness about this path as it winds its quiet way along the stream. There is a tree stump that looks for all the world just like the head of a serpent-like dragon thrusting from the earth, and I wouldn't mind betting that it lies on one of the energy lines (Leys) that snake across the surface of the planet.

I believe in these, but it's not necessary for you to believe in them too. If you are interested in discovering more about Leys, I can highly recommend *The Sun and the Serpent* by Paul Broadhurst as a starting point. It's part history, part travel diary and part spiritual pilgrimage – and 100% funny, inspirational and readable.

Whatever my mood, as I walk the path, I feel my spirits lifting, feel that sense of connection to something greater. It has been proven now that your mood lifts just by going for a walk outside in a park; I would argue that anywhere outside will help! There are many of us that do not have access to a park, many that cannot go outside without help, and many who cannot go outside at all.

Most of us will have been housebound at some point in our lives; think about a time when you were ill and had to stay home, even for just a few days...

... Now think about how you felt when you were well enough to go outside again for the first time; the feeling of relief as you took a lungful of outside air. It is not just a physical reaction, it is a spiritual reaction to connecting once more with nature; it helps you to feel better, optimistic and good inside.

Even if you are indoors, you can still bring this wild energy inside by closing your eyes and imagining you are stood on a hilltop feeling the wind blowing through your outstretched arms, or stood in a rainstorm with the rain pouring down your face. If you want something a little less dramatic, what about seeing yourself sat on a beautiful beach, sun beating down on your back and a cold drink by your side!

Living a spiritual life does not mean praying in the 'hands together, eyes closed' way we were shown when we were young children, but it does mean giving thanks for the good things in our lives, acknowledging when we need to make changes and accepting changes when they happen.

It helps us to focus on what is important, shake off the trivial and move forwards in life, living in the present, rather than remaining trapped in the past.

My life, like yours, has been full of highs and lows, drama and comedy. My spiritual life has taken me up on the downs, into curtained rooms, castle dungeons and hospital wards. At times I have thought I was flying with the angels, at other times I felt deserted and bereft, but always I have known that a life without that sense of connection would feel empty.

Of course, we have to live in the real world too; the world of trying to think of what to have for dinner, of trying to keep our homes in some sort of order despite the best efforts of the kids, of trying to keep our heads above water and somehow, just maybe, having something left over just for us, at the end of the day. It's no good having a direct line to the angels if you don't have anything to eat; everything is a balance, and it's important to get our priorities right, but your spiritual life can help here too. Is it easier to sort out what's most important when you feel cool, calm and collected, or when you are tearing your hair out, beset by anxiety attacks and hurtling from place to place in a vain effort to get at least one thing done! It's not really a choice is it?

I'm apparently an expert at sailing serenely through life; my friends tell me that I'm "so good at coping", "so strong" and have at times held me up as a sort of saint! Well, I'm here to tell you now that the halo has slipped below my (generous) hips and I'm just as scared as everyone else when something happens. I feel a bit like a swan at times: on the surface, I'm gliding along with barely a care, while underneath I'm paddling like mad just to keep going!

When the world goes mad around me, I really need my spiritual life to help and support me. In 2004, I was diagnosed with Breast Cancer and had many months of challenging treatment. My overriding concerns during that time were for my family, particularly my children. I did not want them worrying that I was going to die, so I had to stay upbeat and positive, even when I was feeling really sick and low. It's a funny thing about Cancer, the treatment seems to make you feel worse than the disease, but I would have endured anything to ensure I would still be there for many years to come. Right now, I'm clear, and long may that continue – but if at any time in the future it returns, I know I will have the strength to endure again.

Each of us has our challenges; if we had no challenges, we might not enjoy life. Do you agree with that statement? Take away one challenge and you'll find another to replace it. If money is a challenge right now and you became financially secure overnight, what would you find to give you direction and meaning? That's after you had bought enough shoes of course. When your children grow up and (hopefully) leave home, it can leave a void that is difficult to fill; my third child, my baby girl, has just left school. After two decades of sorting out the school uniform it feels very strange knowing that I no longer have to do it. Working on your inner life, your spiritual life can help to give you that challenge and can also give meaning to your everyday life. The really good news is that if you fit it in around your day, you can do whatever you want with your 'free' time. I've put that in inverted commas because if your life is anything like mine, the concept of free time may be unknown to you. If you are reading this while stood in a bookshop, take it to the counter, pay for it, go home, put your feet up and enjoy some quality me time…

Chapter 2

Probably Nothing

Probably Nothing.

Throughout my life, I have ignored the signs. I expect you have too. I'm not necessarily talking about mystical signs, although I've ignored those with the best of them; these are the real, tangible, physical signs that you need to take some form of action over. I don't want to make assumptions here, but I have a feeling that right now, there is something in your life that you know needs attention, but which you are deliberately ignoring, whether consciously, or subconsciously. It could be any one of a million things; the funny noise coming from the car, or the washing machine; the letters from the bank, the look in someone's eyes...

I have a solution to these things: do not, whatever you do, continue to ignore them.

You don't want to hear this, of course you don't, it might mean a big repair bill, a problem with your finances, or a friend or partner who needs support. The trouble is that if we ignore the signs, things very rarely get better on their own. But here's the thing – if you face up to whatever it is as soon as you possibly can, it can be far less worrying than you thought!

The fear is almost always worse than the reality.

Sometimes we ignore things because we don't take them seriously.

I had this nagging pain in my shoulder that came and went. Nothing major, just one of those sort of 'rotate your shoulder while holding on to it' sort of pains, the sort of pain that comes on after an afternoon gardening, or moving the furniture around. Except that it never came on after any form of exertion; just every now and again, maybe 2 or 3 times a month, while sat up in bed doing the crossword, hardly a strenuous activity! By morning, it had always vanished and I had forgotten about it – until the next time. Like you, I'm a busy sort of person, and a busy person doesn't bother her doctor with trivial nagging pains!

So this nagging pain came and went for almost a year, during 2003 and 2004, before I finally mentioned it to my doctor. I had gone for something completely different, I cannot even remember what that was now, but I do remember that it had been bothering me the previous evening, so was fresh in my mind. I most certainly did not think there was going to be an answer for it, just a mildly patronizing lecture along the lines of 'It's one of the perils of growing older, nagging aches and pains are natural' from my overworked GP. In fact I was apologizing for even bringing it up before I gave her a chance to draw breath and reply!

You could have knocked me down with a feather when she took it seriously and suggested sending me off for a mammogram!

This is how it went...

"By the way, while I'm here, I've had this nagging pain in my shoulder that comes and goes, I don't suppose you have any idea what it might be? ... Probably nothing of course, just getting older I suppose! It's just that it never comes on when I've actually done anything to make it ache – and it only happens at night when I'm sat up in bed in the middle of the *Telegraph* cryptic crossword..."

"How long have you had it?"

"Oh about a year I suppose, on and off, it comes and goes..."

"How often does it happen?"

"About 2 or 3 times a month, it's probably nothing, don't worry..."

"I'm going to send you for a mammogram, just to be on the safe side..."

"A mammogram! But this is my shoulder!"

"Yes, I know – and as you say, it's probably nothing, but as you have had it for almost a year, I think we should investigate it."

Probably nothing... it was my mantra for the next few weeks!

"But if it's nothing, don't worry, I don't want to put anyone to all that trouble, I'm sure it'll go away..."

But the doctor was already writing the referral, it was a done deal. She probably saved my life.

The really, really odd thing was that from the moment I finally told the doctor, the nagging pain vanished, never to return. With hindsight, I'm convinced it was a message from my paternal grandmother 'Big Grandma' to get checked out. We had a 'Big Grandma' and a 'Little Grandma': Big Grandma was big in every way, tall, big boned and with a statuesque figure; Little Grandma, who passed away in April 2012 at 93, was tiny in every way, less than 5 feet tall and with a small frame. Both of them had the biggest hearts though, with family at the heart of whatever they did. Big Grandma had breast cancer back in the early 1960s when treatment was less advanced, and recovery rates much less positive than they are today. She had a mastectomy, and her 'reconstruction' was a grey nylon beanbag shoved into her bra. It was a multipurpose reconstruction – I remember her reaching inside her bra and throwing it to me and my brother to play with sometimes! We would play catch with this makeshift booby, something which I find absolutely incredible now. To go through the trauma of the diagnosis and surgery – and then be relaxed enough about it to let your grandchildren play with the beanbag? I'm truly in admiration of her courage and spirit. I always knew what the beanbag was, I cannot remember now whether I was told, or just overheard something, but I knew she had had a mastectomy, and I knew that the bag was a makeshift booby. My brother on the other hand, only discovered the truth when I was having treatment and we were reminiscing one day. He was horrified! Big Grandma was brilliant; she passed away in 1978, when lung cancer finally overcame her. I miss her still.

I didn't feel alarmed by the prospect of the investigation; I had no lumps and bumps, it was just a nagging shoulder muscle

– wasn't it? The referral duly arrived and I toddled off to the Breast Care Unit at Haslar Hospital in Gosport. (This amazing and utterly brilliant hospital has now been closed, which is a crying shame.)

They were very thorough; I had my 'Squashogram' (every time I have a check up, I worry about the fire alarms going off while I'm being held firm by the squashography machine!), and then went to see a Nurse Practitioner to have it analyzed. I explained what had been happening and the nurse had a good feel for lumps – there were none. There was a tiny sore patch, so she performed a needle aspiration to draw off some cells, the results were ready in about an hour, and were clear. However, they weren't ready to let me go just yet; an Ultrasound was required – 'Just to be on the safe side.'

... And there it was: a tiny opaque sphere, deep within the breast tissue. Something so tiny that it surely had to be completely insignificant? Apparently not. They didn't like the look of it, and booked me in for a Core Biopsy for the following week. "Probably nothing," she said. "Just to be on the safe side."

I didn't feel even the faintest twinge of alarm; how could anything that small be in any way threatening?

The core biopsy was taken; the mantra was duly repeated: 'Probably nothing'... two weeks later I went back for the pathology results and it turned out that actually, it was... something... and the something might just be threatening – but not very threatening; whatever it was, it was in the very early stages they thought – but I would need a lumpectomy to remove it. I was more than happy with this; I wanted the little blighter gone!

My lumpectomy was scheduled for Halloween week in 2004; I love Halloween, I love pumpkins and I love fairy lights – so I took Halloween, pumpkin-shaped, orange battery-powered fairy lights into the hospital with me, and put them out on the table over my bed. It still seems logical to me now, although it may have appeared ever so slightly barking mad to others. The lumpectomy was performed and I left the hospital after a few days, still completely unconcerned.

The pathology results took a further two weeks to materialize; it seemed that the entire world was getting their results at that clinic; it was packed. A large seating area was surrounded on three sides by closed doors, the consulting rooms. A veritable army of nursing staff and counselors were conspicuous around the room, their eyes scanning the throng as though assessing who would be able to cope and who would need extra support. There were silent, worried women, and chatty women trying not to look worried. Husbands, partners and loved ones sat closely to their women, trying to be supportive and not knowing what to say. I spotted a familiar face or two, women who had been on the ward with me, also now awaiting their fate, including Lorraine, who had been in the next bed, and who had become a friend. There was an air of forced cheerfulness, a faint desperation in the air, as though the very act of cheerfulness could ward off whatever waited behind the closed doors.

My name was called; a door opened, and Phil and I went in and sat down.

Behind the desk, a doctor was waiting; he confirmed a few details to make sure I was the right patient and then, with no preamble, he uttered the following sentence...

"Mrs. Jones, I'm afraid it's not good news. The pathology results show you have Breast Cancer, a type called DCIS, which stands for Ductal Carcinoma in Situ. It's category 3, aggressive and multifocal, you will need chemotherapy, radiotherapy, a mastectomy, possibly reconstruction and then drugs such as Tamoxifen. Do you have any questions?"

Questions? I thought this was supposed to be 'Probably Nothing'! As if from a distance I heard myself saying:

"We've got tickets to go and see The Darkness (bestselling rock band at that time) at Wembley next month. Can I still go?"

There was a distinct pause. I remember this quite clearly... and a sort of giggly gasp from the nurse standing guard in the corner.

"Er... I don't see why not? Umm..."

I let him off the hook with a sigh. "OK, so I presume by multi-focal you mean there's more than one of the things?"

"Yes," he was back on familiar territory. "We have identified three cancers in the breast." More silence.

"... And category 3 means...?"

"Ah – yes, the categories go up on level of threat if you like, from 1, which is the lowest, to 4, which is the highest."

"So what happens now?"

He talked about the coming months, the chemotherapy would be the first hurdle, then surgery; but first I would see the Breast Care Nurses to talk things through and support me. I was strangely calm, still not alarmed and I thanked him and left the room, followed by poor Phil, who was really suffering. I have always felt that the husbands and partners of women with breast cancer should have proper support; it's getting better, but there is still much work to do.

Back in the seating area, I could feel all the eyes on me as I came out of the door, trying to assess what my outcome had been. There was no sign of my friend, but I could hear something of a commotion coming from behind one of the other doors, and it sounded familiar. I walked over to the door and asked the nurse outside if Lorraine was inside.

"You can't go in there!" she said, but I was already turning the door handle. Lorraine was there, in a state of visible distress. "Lorraine! It's only me – are you OK?" Stupid bloody question as she plainly wasn't OK. "How did you get on?" we both asked the question simultaneously, but we both knew the answers. We hugged each other tightly; sometimes it's easier to talk to someone, share with someone, the thing that is frightening you, if you are both experiencing it at the same time. We supported each other right through the whole process, and then, ultimately, we got on with our lives. It's not that we fell out, just that we needed each other for a fixed period and then, somehow, we didn't need each other any more. We were part of a process that naturally completed.

Anyway, it seemed now that 'Probably Nothing' was no longer my mantra. My new mantra was 'Survive'.

I was understandably concerned about telling the kids; James had just turned 16, Matt was almost 12 and Holly was 8. I knew I had to be strong for them; I didn't want any element of 'doom and gloom' permeating our close-knit family. I told each of them separately, reassuring them that I would be absolutely fine, although in the short-term it might be difficult as the treatment would make me ill, and of course I was probably going to lose my hair, but I'd try not to scare them with my bald head! James and Holly were fine, but Matt was more tricky to pin down. I thought he must be worried that I might die… but no, when I finally cornered him it seemed that his main area of concern was that I might embarrass him if my wig blew away in the wind! I did my best to allay his fears while trying not to laugh! Kids have a way of bringing you down to earth.

I was also worried about how my surgery might affect my relationship with Phil. Although I had complete faith in his love and support, I wasn't sure how he would feel about the mastectomy and reconstruction. The man who loved my 'baby bag' was also completely unconcerned about me losing bits of myself… "I married you, not your tits…" he said, enveloping me in a bear hug when I raised the issue. It might sound a bit… erm… direct… but it was what I needed to hear! Phil has always been absolutely there for me, whenever I need him. I feel absolutely blessed that we met, and cherish every moment we spend together.

One thing that took me entirely by surprise was the reaction by other people to my cancer. I'm only mentioning this in case you know someone who has recently been diagnosed... please treat them normally! There were a significant few who felt unable to talk to me when they discovered I had cancer... apparently they couldn't cope, didn't know what to say – basically I had to feel sorry for them. I'm sorry? *I* had to feel sorry for *them*? Who had the cancer! I am over this now, but I was really angry about it at the time; after all, I was the one walking around with no hair! It seems to be a common reaction too, but people with cancer are still the same people. There's no need to find anything different to say, just talk about what you would normally discuss! They'll have ups and downs, good days and bad days and it will make a real difference to know that you are there when they need you.

One group that I had no concerns about were our five kitties. While I was ill, they temporarily suspended all hostilities between themselves to help look after me. There are countless stories of pets who seem to know when someone is ill; ours were certainly aware of how ill I was. I would be lying in bed quietly twitching and trying to rest and five furry bodies would be squashed up against me! The only time their attentions caused a problem was the notorious 'Sofa Incident'.

It was the smell we noticed; a nasty musty smell. I put it down to Phil's feet, or maybe the cushion covers... I washed the covers but the smell still lingered. My sense of smell was exceptionally sensitive when I was having chemotherapy, so initially I thought it was only me smelling it, but over the next few days it got worse and worse. After a couple of weeks had passed I decided I had to do something; I was convinced now it was the covers on the sofa so I thought I would wash them... As I removed the upright back cushions to remove the covers, something moved... there was something there, what was it...? "Oh YUK... PHIL...!!!" I remember shrieking for him to come quickly; there was a little present from one of the cats down the back of the sofa, a headless (and very, very long dead) rat, which had obviously been decomposing for some time! Now I'm not frightened of rodents, alive or dead, but I was concerned about the germs from this particular specimen, especially in view of my chemically compromised immune system, so I called the home insurance company and said I wanted to make a claim. They were most sympathetic and sent out a cleaning team, but despite their best efforts they were unable to remove the aroma of decomposing rodent and after a couple of attempts they gave us the cash to buy a new sofa! That was definitely a result; it gave me something to focus on and take my mind off the ghastly chemo. Whenever I think about it, it also reminds me of my somewhat limited diet at that time; I had gone off food in a big way and was surviving on a healthy mix of satsumas and Maltesers (malt balls), yum.

Following my breast cancer diagnosis, I was back and forth to the hospital on a regular basis to discuss my treatment. The chemotherapy was to start immediately, and surgery would follow in 2005 once I had recovered sufficiently from being poisoned. I knew that in all probability I would lose my hair, so being a control freaky Capricorn, I knew I had to be in charge of that. I have had very long hair for most of my life and one of my greatest fears had always been losing it. Facing that fear head on would be my first challenge; I decided take control and to have it cut very short before the first treatment; to bolster my spirits I did it for the charity *Children in Need*, raising around £900 from friends, family and folks at the local pub. Two of my friends from school made time in their busy lives to travel down to Portsmouth and come with me to the hairdresser. It was great to see them again, and with all the catching up we had to do, I had no time to feel sorry for myself. Actually, I quite liked the new look – although I have once more grown my hair again now. I find it easier to manage and I am absolutely NOT going to be grey! I think purple is a great color!

I was pretty phobic about throwing up, and everything I had heard about chemotherapy made me think I would be vomiting pretty much constantly (It's not necessarily true; I made it through without hurling once.), so I made sure that I had plenty of anti-sickness medication.

The first treatment was OK; I felt a bit off color for a day or so, and then I was back to normal, so we went Christmas shopping. I saw a nice jumper in one shop and went to try it on – and as I removed the jumper I was wearing… most of my hair came off too, in one lump. I stood staring at it in the corner of the changing room for a minute; it looked for all the world like a deflated hedgehog, spiky brown tufts in a sad little heap. Nothing I could do to change it though. I looked in the mirror and felt my head; there still seemed to be a fair amount left, enough that I wouldn't scare the Christmas shoppers! The surreal nature of my situation suddenly hit me and I started giggling; I decided not to try on the jumper after all, just in case the rest came off, and carefully replaced my own top. I couldn't face taking the pile of hair away with me, so I left it in a corner of the changing room – god knows what the sales staff must have thought!

Phil looked at me as I came out of the changing rooms. "Was it OK?" he asked. "Actually I didn't get that far," I replied and explained, "I think the rest had better come off tonight – have you got Kev's number on you?" Kev and his wife Sue are two of our closest friends – and Kev keeps his head close shaven. "I want the rest shaved off tonight!" Phil threw me a worried glance, "Are you sure about this?" "Absolutely sure," I replied. I could not bear the thought of the chemotherapy taking away my hair, but if I chose to do it, well, that was a completely different thing. I had the headscarves and the wigs ready and waiting…

That was an odd Saturday night; sitting in the kitchen having what was left of my hair shaved off… and then immediately going back to long hair with a wig! I discovered very quickly that I could not tolerate the wigs; I had loved wearing wigs to parties and thought it would be quite entertaining changing hairstyles and colors whenever I fancied for a while, but they irritated my scalp so I opted for a variety of headscarves instead. I only wore the wigs if I absolutely had to; I used to do tarot and angel Card readings for people and I would wear the wig for these, not wanting to scare folks; but I remember one particular occasion when two ladies came round for a reading. After they had left, I caught sight of myself in the mirror and realized that I had forgotten to fasten it at the back; the two straps were hanging down around my ears! What on earth must they have thought!

Chemotherapy has a cumulative effect, so you can become more debilitated with each treatment. The couple of days feeling a bit 'off' after the first treatment escalated to a full week in bed feeling ghastly by treatment number 5. It wasn't helped by the state of my veins and skin. My veins collapsed after the first treatment; my blood failed to recover and the second treatment had to be delayed. When I was eventually ready for number 2, they had to insert a PICC (Peripherally Inserted Central Catheter) Line in order to administer the drugs. This is a very thin and flexible line (it felt like balloon plastic), which is inserted through a vein in the upper arm and which follows the vein around directly into the heart. It means that there are no painful episodes while the nurses try to find a vein when you go for your appointments; it should be a simple task to initially insert it – but of course it wasn't for me. I ended up badly bruised and battered after a lengthy spell on the couch while the expert technicians battled to find a vein that they could use. I'm conscious that I might sound like a bit of a disaster area, but I cannot help the facts – and the fact was that everything they did affected me badly. The PICC line was brilliant… but the tape to stick it down reacted horribly with my skin. Within a few days I had a severe allergic rash; the nurses likened the effect to being burned with aircraft fuel. It was the same with every sticky tape they tried; I was back and forth to the hospital almost daily to try and resolve the issue – but ultimately they had to bandage it in place without an adhesive, something which carried another risk. If the line is not secured, it can be sucked into the body completely… and then it's major surgery to retrieve it! We eventually identified one brand of tape (Hypafix) that I seemed to be OK with… but this year I have become sensitive to that too. Not sure what happens if I need sticking together now!

Throughout chemotherapy, although I was really grateful to have my family around me, I also valued my time alone. This has always been such a busy, happy house; I still wanted my children to be able to bring their friends home, but sometimes you need to be on your own. The kids were so comfortable about my appearance that they would sometimes forget that a) their friends might feel just slightly spooked by the sight of a bald woman reclining on the sofa as they trooped past me to get to the stairs, or b) I might not want to be seen without my headscarf. I got into the habit of retiring early to get some peace and quiet when I needed it; no drama, just 'I'm off to bed now'. I might not be going to sleep though; our bedroom is my sanctuary where I can completely relax. I can read, listen to music, meditate, catch up with my favorite telly… I resisted having a TV in the bedroom for years and finally gave in about 5 years before. It's not been the root of all evil that I imagined, but rather a friend on the wall who only speaks up when I need them. If I'm feeling under the weather and have to stay in bed, it helps me feel connected to the world. If there's a program I want to watch that nobody else does, I can relax in peace without (hopefully) constant interruptions from the offspring!

Now this is where it gets slightly spooky, because of a wish I made. You have probably heard of Cosmic Ordering, or something like it. It's the theory that you can get what you want in life by ordering it from the universe, a bit like buying stuff online. I'll talk about this in more detail in a later chapter, but up until then, I didn't really buy into it. I might be 'into' all this spiritual and cosmic stuff, but I'm not daft and I certainly didn't believe that you could influence events your way simply by wishing for something!

This is what happened to change my mind.

You have to understand that back then I was seriously overweight. I had been really skinny as a teenager, but years on the pill, three children and a serious chocolate addiction had piled on the pounds and by 2004 I weighed about 16.5 stones (231 pounds). I was in complete denial about my size despite having to buy larger and larger clothes; I still have a trouser suit I bought in October 2004, it's UK size 24. The only part of my body I really hated was my stomach; Phil called it my 'Baby Bag', a ghastly overhanging fold of flesh that I was horribly self-conscious about. Phil didn't mind, and he certainly didn't think he was being insulting with his pet name for my droopy tummy, but I really, really hated it. I could only wear waist-high control knickers to try and contain it; no skimpy sexy undies for me!

So one night, about three weeks before I went for that original mammogram, we were sat watching telly, and something comes on to do with cosmetic surgery. I cannot remember what it was now, it's not important. What is important is that I turned to Phil and said,

"I would do ANYTHING to get a tummy tuck, absolutely ANYTHING!"

We were pretty skint (broke) and there was no way we could afford to pay for any cosmetic surgery, so it felt completely out of reach.

"I would do ANYTHING to get a tummy tuck, absolutely ANYTHING!"

The sheer unhappiness, pent-up desperation about how I looked, the feeling that a tummy tuck was the answer to all my weight problems, all that passion was concentrated in one single wish.

"I would do ANYTHING to get a tummy tuck, absolutely ANYTHING!"

… And the universe heard me, and granted my wish.

It's complicated; even I think this is nuts, but there's no denying the fact that within months of that impassioned plea, I got my tummy tuck… in a way I could never have imagined, in a way I didn't even know was possible at that time.

The chemotherapy had dragged on over the winter, each dose leaving me feeling more debilitated. I kept in touch with Lorraine, whose own treatment was progressing, but our treatments were out of sync because it was taking me so long to recover, so we would phone each other regularly and would meet up for lunch occasionally. One day I called for her at her home and she was full of excitement.

"I've been looking at reconstruction methods online and found something amazing!" She dragged me in to look at something on the computer. "What do you think of that then!"

On the screen was information relating to something called a 'TRAM (Transverse Rectus Abdominus Myocutaneous) Flap Reconstruction'. The surgeon uses tissue from the abdomen to make a new 'breast' – I wanted a tummy tuck – why not get it on the NHS! I didn't make the connection immediately; it was only a couple of weeks later that I remembered my wish. I now believe that it was the complete surrender to the fates, as well as the passion in the plea that 'activated' the wish, if you like. After all, all of us make wishes all the time, but not all of them are fulfilled.

These days I most definitely am more careful about HOW I wish for things.

With the chemotherapy completed, I went to meet my plastic surgeon, an absolutely amazing man and nothing short of a miracle worker in my opinion. I remember walking in and sitting down and being asked if I had given any thought to the question of reconstruction. I most certainly had! I told him that I wanted a TRAM flap reconstruction, that I had read about it on the Internet, and that was the only thing that would do for me. He was really positive, even though I could tell he was a little taken aback by my eagerness! There were many things to consider; it was a complicated procedure, with a prolonged recovery time, and things that could go wrong. I was adamant, though, this was what I wanted. He explained that although he would do his best, I might end up with unevenly sized breasts if there was not enough tissue to work with. I pointed out that I had enough surplus tissue round my middle to start a breast bank! That made him laugh!

The date of the surgery was arranged: 25th April 2005. Phil and I decided to have a few days away on our own just prior to that. We stayed in the wonderful 'Bath Paradise House' hotel in Bath where we were beautifully looked after by both the staff and George, the resident cat! We had a lovely time, shopping in Bath, enjoying the pubs and restaurants and made time to visit the remains of the massive henge monument at Stanton Drew. I loved it there, wandering around with my pendulum, tracking energy lines and soaking up the atmosphere. It's not anywhere near as well-known as Stonehenge and was completely deserted on the day we went. Apart from the cows that is; I have an irrational fear of cows and I'm sure they know… I would carefully wander away from the cows towards a different area of the henge, and after a couple of minutes, I would catch sight of them trying to look nonchalant while creeping up on me. One of the games I would play with my friends as a child involved one child stood with their back to the other players, while they tried to quietly creep up on them. Every now and again, the lone child would suddenly turn around and cry, "Wolf!" All the others then had to stand as still as statues; anyone caught moving was out. Now imagine playing it with cows and you will understand why I felt nervous.

We also visited the Roman Baths in um… Bath. Most of what you see has been lovingly reconstructed by the Victorians, but it doesn't really matter, the place has an incredible aura about it, even when crammed with tourists! If you are anywhere that might be considered sacred, try to separate your ego mind (more on this in later chapters) from your subconscious to send out 'feelers' to see what's out there... I would have loved to have been able to spend some time in there alone, but I guess that's fairly unlikely, so you have to make do with what you can manage. The original spring, sacred to Sulis Minerva, still has a somewhat unearthly air, as the hot water bubbles up from deep within the earth.

I'm digressing I know (I'm an expert) but there is a point here. After months of frankly exhausting treatment and the prospect of life-threatening surgery before me, I needed to recharge my spiritual batteries. I also wanted to spend some quality time with Phil; I cannot thank him enough for everything he did to look after me – and for putting up with me when I was very grumpy and ill.

The day after returning from Bath, I went into the hospital for my mastectomy and reconstruction. There are a few things that really stand out from that first day, the day before the actual operation. I've always had a slightly odd sense of humor and it certainly helps sometimes! All the women had something of an obsession with 'white cotton underpants'; this was because they were apparently the only safe thing to wear in theatre. I took a brand new pack of six with me, but only brought home four as I donated two pairs to ladies who had not realized they would not be allowed to wear anything else – and who wants to go naked under a hospital gown? They're revealing enough as it is! As each new patient arrived, they were quizzed on their possession of white cotton pants and as each of us went to theatre, everyone would ask (patients and nursing staff), "Have you got your white cotton pants on?" It was a ritual passed on from patient to patient, like a never ending chain letter. However, the first thing I had to have done was my photographs. The most undignified and bizarre pictures I have ever had taken... of the bit between my neck, and the top of my thighs. Lovely. It's so the surgeons have reference points when they're rebuilding you, but it's completely surreal standing there in an office while a man in a white coat takes photos of your bits... especially when you loathe your flabby tummy! Still, I thought, last time... it'll be gone tomorrow. Once the photos are done, it's back to the ward and a battery of blood tests (a real challenge with my veins!), then a visit from the anesthetist to discuss my impending snooze. I quite like the snooze – or rather I like the floaty bit when you are coming round, it feels to me like sleeping in the sun under a blanket when you come back from the beach as a child... I put in my requests for extra anti-sickness drugs and ask that I'm allowed to sleep for a bit afterwards. He looks at me a little oddly, something which I only understood later.

My surgeon arrives, with his Senior House Officer (SHO). They talk me through everything again and I sign the forms. No going back now. The surgery involves (sorry if you are squeamish, just don't read this bit!) one team of surgeons to perform the mastectomy, then the Plastic Surgery team coming in to do the reconstruction. Look it up online if you want the gory details, but basically, they take a section of the abdominal tissue, keep a blood supply at one end and sort of push it up and under the abdominal skin until it emerges in the right place. They then shape it and sort out more blood supply before closing it all up again.

Before I go to sleep that night, I pray that I'll come through it all safely, but I am strangely comfortable with it. Not once did I ever feel even slightly scared.

In the morning, up bright and early, I ask the nurse where I am on the list for the day... she throws me a sharp look and says, "You ARE the list for today!" Ah.

The SHO arrives with a black marker pen. "I just need to draw on you," he says. "We need to make sure we are operating on the right breast!" I laugh, "That's the left breast of course!" He looks puzzled. "The right breast... " he says, looking down at my notes. "No, the LEFT breast..." I insist, after all, I should know! "I'm sure it was the right breast... oh hang on – do you mean YOUR left?" God help us, I would have laughed if it hadn't been just a teeny bit scary! I let him draw on me – it looks wonderful. Thick black lines and arrows on my torso. The trolley arrives and I climb aboard; everyone waves me on and wishes me luck as I am wheeled away to theatre...

Apparently I was in theatre for around nine hours, apparently I then woke up, was deemed to be OK, and wheeled off to the high dependency unit. I don't remember much at all about the next few days, just faces floating in and out as my family visited. I'd open my eyes and see Phil, then close them for what felt like a few moments and he would have been replaced by my mum. It was a very strange experience, full of dreams of sunshine and sand, and intermittent appalling pain. The only conversation I recall was with a nurse who didn't know what baby wipes were, although I may have dreamt it.

I know now that it's necessary for the patient to be kept sedated and closely monitored in the days following this sort of major surgery; they need to be sure the reconstruction is bonding and healing, and that they can keep the pain to bearable levels. As I gradually became more aware, the pain was most certainly something that could not be ignored.

The new 'breast' was fine, although I felt like a weird sort of octopus because of all the drains hanging out of me, I think there were seven altogether, tubes protruding from inside my body and leading to collections bags. It was the tummy tuck that was the issue; I was virtually cut in half in order to remove the horrid flabby tummy. The scar covers all of my abdomen at the front and goes around each side, just stopping short of my back. I had not realized just how much you use your abdominal muscles, all the time, from shifting about while lying down, or seated, to getting up and moving about.

Trying to raise myself from a lying to a sitting position was excruciating. I could not do it unaided; two nurses had to help me. It felt as though I was being cut in half all over again, but this time without an anesthetic. After about five days, they wanted me to try walking; I asked for a walking frame, but they laughingly refused, reassuring me that I could do it, and that I would be up and about in no time! It felt as though I would never be independent again at that point, but I knew I had to try. The first time I made it out of bed and up through the ward to the loo, everyone wanted to talk to me, to offer their support.

The wards at Haslar Hospital in Gosport were of the 'Nightingale' style, a long room, with beds either side and a nurses' station at one end. All the patients were women having breast cancer treatment or goiter operations; the support we were able to offer each other was fantastic – I believe that this is in part because of the layout. We could all see each other, we all had similar issues, and we all talked to each other. We even had a Mexican themed party one night, decorating the ward using inflated gloves for balloons, and a variety of trays and assorted paraphernalia for hats and bunting! I compared this with a later trip to the hospital when I was in a small room of four beds in the Plastic Surgery Ward, four women with different issues and not much in common. One of the women was there to have her breasts enlarged; although she was nice enough, her continual chatter about how big she wanted them and what her boyfriend would say felt a little tactless when I was there because of breast cancer! After a couple of days, everyone else had gone home apart from me and I became very depressed and tearful and asked to go back to the Breast Cancer Care Ward. The nurses fully supported me and I was moved within a couple of hours; it felt like going home.

I would like to offer my heartfelt thanks to all the nursing staff at Haslar Hospital; they were amazing, the most patient, attentive and caring group of individuals. The surgeons worked miracles, the nurses worked magic.

My recovery from the surgery was slow, as expected, but after almost two weeks in the hospital, I came home, on a sunny Friday afternoon in May.

At this point in my story, I have to tell you that I consider myself to be reasonably intelligent... and utterly stupid! When I made that heartfelt wish to the universe –

I would do ANYTHING to get a tummy tuck!

– I had no idea how it could possibly be accomplished, but I was absolutely rock solid sure that it would be the answer to all my prayers. It would, in one stroke, solve all my self-image issues, turn me into a happy, successful – and incredibly thin and attractive – woman.

I went into the operating theatre weighing 16½ stones and was a size 20–22.

I honestly thought I would emerge as a perfect size 12.

While we were spending those few days away in Bath, I treated myself to a new outfit to go home in from the hospital. I decided not to go too mad and buy a size 12, although I thought that was probably being pessimistic, so I bought a size 14 summer skirt, and a couple of size 14 cotton T-shirts, just to be going on with. I even chatted cheerfully to the sales assistants in the shop about how much slimmer I was going to be – so there was probably no point in me trying anything on; I was really looking forward to shopping for clothes when I was fully recovered!

I had it all packed and ready for Phil to bring in for me to go home in...

Thankfully, the awful abdominal pain from the tummy tuck wound made me a little worried about wearing a skirt. I wasn't sure if it would cut in and make things more painful, so I asked Phil to bring in one of my 'old' summer dresses too.

It's a good job I did.

Of course I wasn't a size 12 – or anywhere near it! While I was completely focused on that flabby tummy, I had forgotten the rest of me; my tummy might be flatter, but yes, my bum still looked big, from any angle! To say that I was 'disappointed' when I tried on my new skirt is an understatement... Even though I was seriously overweight, I had managed to avoid ever truly acknowledging it, it was just baby weight, just my tummy. It's amazing how I was able to so completely fool myself, to see a completely different person when I looked in the mirror.

So I put on my old dress, made my emotional farewells to the ward, and Phil drove me home. My ability to deceive myself hadn't stopped with my appearance either. I thought I could go home and pick up where I left off, if not that day, then certainly within a couple of days, but of course I couldn't. I was in so much pain, not helped by managing to slide most of the way down the stairs within half an hour of arriving home, that all I was capable of was throwing painkillers down my throat and crying. That first night home was probably the worst night of my life; without the safety net of the nurse at the end of the ward, I was incredibly anxious; I couldn't lie flat because of the huge healing wound pulling, and I couldn't get comfortable in any other position either. I slept fitfully, propped up on cushions and at some point towards dawn had the most awful nightmare about never healing from this god-awful agony.

Everything looks brighter, however, in the morning, and at this point I made another monumentally stupid decision. I would go shopping... and following the shopping, we would go to a barbecue, at a friend's house.

I must have been off my head; what was I thinking?!

Unable to sit, lie or stand comfortably, taking very strong pain relief, just out of the hospital following major surgery, in huge amounts of pain – it's obvious isn't it? Just get on with things, don't want to disappoint anyone, don't want to let anyone down. I even considered offering to drive so Phil could have a drink – but thankfully, I thought better of it!

We drove to the local supermarket, where I took control of a mobility scooter to get me around… I can tell you two things about them: 1. People treat you as though you have a mental deficiency if you are driving one, and 2. They don't go nearly fast enough. Following a tense hour of shopping – I don't know who was more terrified, me or Phil, we went home where I 'relaxed' for an hour (for 'relaxed', read half lay on the sofa groaning in pain and trying not to stress over whether poor Phil was folding the washing in my preferred manner) and then we went out again, to the barbecue, where I sat uncomfortably in a chair in the garden and froze half to death. It was only the second weekend of May.

By Monday morning, I thought I should be able to accompany Phil on the school run, so off we went, Phil driving the nine miles to Buriton Primary School. As we stood at the gate chatting with some of the other parents, one of them pointed at my white T-shirt and calmly asked if "it was meant to be doing that?" As I looked down, to my horror I realized that there was blood every-where, pouring from the wound underneath the reconstruction. We rushed home, called the hospital, and then drove to the hospital to see a nurse, who thought it was probably just a pocket of blood that had built up, would leak out and then stop. Nothing to worry about. We drove home again.

However, it didn't stop, and within days I was back in the hospital with a serious infection in the wound under the recon-struction; more surgery required immediately.

My wonderful surgeon had done his best to make the recon-structed breast as large as possible, and believe me, I had enough tummy to start a 'Breast Bank'. The new booby was monstrous, so large I was calling it 'Jordan'!

I was also discovering that it was heavier than the natural breast had been; heavier, and of course, off to one side, so that I was off balance. My back was killing me. I asked the surgeon if he could reduce the size and he replied that of course he could – but they needed to kill the infection first. I had to stay in the hospital for a further week while they gave me blood transfusions and antibiotics, and then they sent me home again, this time with an open wound that required daily dressing and a 'Penrose Drain', which allows all the nasty stuff to drain into the dressings… which then smell absolutely vile. I had to keep this on for a month before going back in for yet more surgery.

Under these trying circumstances, it would be natural to rest as much as possible and submit to the daily ministrations of the nurses… but oh no, not me.

I decided what we all needed was a holiday!

Can I just say now, that Phil is a saint to even put up with me? Any normal human being would have had me committed for even thinking about going away...

We packed up the Shogun and went down to Padstow, in Cornwall, for a relaxing few days travelling between the local surgery and the crazy golf. We couldn't stay in our usual apartment as it was so last minute, and because it was Half Term (school break) we couldn't even get close to the harbor area – which is completely flat – but found a tiny new-build house to rent on the steep slopes as you drive in and out of town. Convenient for Tesco (supermarket), but nothing else. I was completely incapable of walking any distance on the flat area, let alone up and down the hill, so Phil drove me and the kids down, and then went back up and parked… and either climbed back to get the car to collect me, or found a taxi to ferry me back to the house. It was hardly relaxing – and then, as it was a Bank Holiday weekend, the surgery was closed, so Phil had to change my ghastly stinky dressings.

I don't think I had really thought it through.

That month really was a low point. I felt about a hundred years old as I staggered around, constantly aware of the rotting smell coming from the dressings, constantly on the look out for leakage through my clothes. Eventually, after the next lot of surgery, I finally began to heal properly. The new 'breast' had been halved in size (!), the abdominal pain had gradually eased and I began to think and behave like a normal human being again, well, at least what passes for normal in this house. The 'Cancer' word slowly receded into the background, as the physical scars faded. I had a few other minor operations to tidy things up and also to deal with a hernia along that pesky tummy tuck, and so far (everything crossed) I'm OK.

There were so many strange moments along the way; at times I felt like a bizarre form of 'Topless Glamour Model' as so many people seemed to need (or want) to look at my newly reformed boobs. I remember at one point waking up in the hospital to see my surgeon approaching; "Would you mind if some of my colleagues had a look at your reconstruction?" "Erm… no, that's fine," I replied, not quite expecting the 12 different surgeons and doctors who suddenly materialized to gaze intently at my chest. It would have been nice if they had been as interested in my face, mind. Long after I'm gone, my breasts will live on, up there in hyperspace, to show student doctors and women considering the surgery what is possible. I was very lucky to have such a fabulous result; I tell folks that I have a better matching pair now than before the cancer – I can wear anything I like and you really cannot tell I have had a full mastectomy at all. Brilliant.

In one of my 'Crap' drawers – every home has at least one, full of oddments you are keeping for no good reason… Christmas cracker gifts, seeds in handwritten envelopes, sewing kits from hotel rooms etc… Anyway, in one of these drawers I have one of those round adhesive patches that the nurses stick on you prior to hooking you up to a heart monitor.

It was about a year after the 'big' operation; I had gone back to have the first stage of nipple reconstruction surgery and was back on the Breast Cancer Care Ward. The curtains were drawn around the bed, and I was stood by the bed, wearing only a pair of the obligatory white cotton pants. Two men were kneeling on the floor in front of me brandishing the inevitable black marker pen; my miracle worker and his SHO trying to decide where my new nipple should go... not helped by me giggling all the time! Well, I ask you, what is a girl supposed to do when she is faced with two handsome men kneeling before her almost-naked self? It still makes me laugh now! In the end, they gave up, gave me the sticker and told me to go to the bathroom, to look in the mirror... and stick it on where I thought my nipple should go! I just had to keep it afterwards.

Incidentally, stage two of the nipple reconstruction process involves a nursing sister who tattoos a nice wobbly pink circle onto the retextured skin. I didn't fancy a wobbly pink circle; after everything I had been through, I wanted something spectacular! My lovely surgeon wrote me a letter to give to my tattoo artist explaining that it was OK, it wasn't a real breast, and after a further year to allow the scarring to settle down, I went to one of the best tattoo artists in the world for the work. I have a shocking pink dragon, which winds back and forth in a circular labyrinth pattern, perfect in every tiny scale on his body; much, much better than a wobbly pink circle! I think the tattoo artist was a bit freaked out by it though; because the reconstructive work is so good, it's difficult to believe it's not a real breast – poor chap kept asking me to reassure him that I couldn't feel anything!

There is one person I haven't mentioned when discussing the surgery: my anesthetist. He was very patient with my constant nagging over anti-sickness medication and attentive to how I was feeling at all times. He talked me gently into uncon-sciousness on the occasion that they could not find any vein at all to administer the anesthetic and I had to have gas instead. The mask and the feeling of suffocation was making me panic, and it was only his voice that stopped me from going completely crazy and ripping off the mask. I was in and out of theatre quite frequently and it was good to have his constant presence; I thought of him as my Angel of Sleep. They always had the radio on in theatre; on one occasion, *The Boys Are Back In Town* by Thin

Lizzy (one of my favorite bands) was playing and I asked if we could delay the big sleep until the guitar solo at the end had finished. As I drifted off, I heard one of the nurses saying to him, "Is that supposed to be an air guitar you're playing?" and I fell asleep laughing at the image it presented.

I'm writing this in May 2013, exactly eight years since that dreadful time after I first came home from the hospital and then had the infection; in some ways cancer feels like a lifetime away, so much has happened since then. And in other ways it's with me every minute of every day. I say this in a positive way; I believe that having breast cancer is one of the greatest blessings I have received in my life. I do not let it 'define' me in any way, but it has taught me to appreciate life and love and everything I have in ways that might never have happened otherwise. It's helped me through all sorts of situations because it encourages me to always, always look for the positive side of things first, and to face up, and deal with things before they have a chance to become bigger issues. This brings me neatly full circle, back to the beginning of this chapter.

How many times have you said: "It's probably nothing" and walked away? How many times have you thought: "I must see to that... " and left it? How many of you reading this are experiencing symptoms that might be worrying you, or know someone who is worrying about their health, but who has not been to see a doctor?

Here are your options.

1. You visit your doctor and discover that you were right, there is nothing to worry about. Result? Peace of mind. In this case, the quicker you visit the doctor, the faster you get that peace of mind.
2. You visit your doctor and discover that there is something that needs dealing with, but the sooner you go, the better off you will be.

3. You don't visit your doctor and worry yourself about it for a lot longer than necessary before eventually it becomes apparent that there was probably nothing to worry about. You may be left with nagging concerns that don't recede.

4. You leave it and leave it until visiting your doctor is a necessity and there really is something to be concerned about. Result? Worrying times ahead...

Trust me, the fear is always worse than the reality; the discovery that I would need chemotherapy made me very nervous – not because of the possibility of losing my hair, but because of the probability that at some point during the process, I would throw up. Everyone knows that chemo makes you vomit...? Actually I didn't. There are loads of antinausea, anti-emetic drugs these days, you just have to ask for them, which I did, until everyone was sick of me asking! I've had a bit of a phobia about being sick since 1983; I had an unfortunate incident with a pushbike and a gravelly road which led to me having to have my jaws wired together for six weeks – well, anyone would be scared of being sick under those circumstances. I'm over it now, really.

'It's probably nothing' could be holding you back, keeping you in a place you don't find comfortable. 'It's probably nothing' causes sleepless nights, anxiety and stress. Facing up to the situation will help you in many ways, one of the most important of which is putting you firmly in the driving seat. If you feel in control of a situation, rather than spiraling out of control, then your mind will be easier, and you can more objectively consider the best courses of action. In the chapter on your Inner Voice, I'll try and help you with that.

One of the things that really helped me through breast cancer, and continues to help me, every day, is meditation – no, don't make a face – you won't need the loincloth, and that's what I'm going to talk about next.

Chapter 3

Throw Away Your Loincloth!

The Truth about Meditation

Do you have time to sit on a mountaintop for hours, wearing a loincloth, chanting the mystical 'Ommmmmmmmmmmmmmm'?

No, I don't either, you are joking aren't you?

I find that little everyday things have a tendency to creep into my mind all the time... I find myself wondering if the washing machine has finished yet, or whether I remembered to take something out of the freezer for dinner! It took me years to discover a foolproof technique, but you don't have to wait... you can cancel the order for that loincloth now!

Meditation is generally agreed to be one of the key skills on any personal and spiritual development path, but there are many people who are absolutely convinced they cannot 'do' meditation, for many reasons. So how would you feel if I told you that you can meditate, that you are doing it all the time already, and that all you have to do is sharpen that skill just a little in order to be able to achieve all those lovely serene benefits you thought were beyond your reach!

When I was training to be a Spiritual Healer, I was required to meditate for at least an hour every day... Now I have to tell you that while I love my family to bits, they are not exactly quiet, and the combination of noise from their chatter, washing machines, dryers, TVs, game consoles, computers and music do not exactly make for a tranquil atmosphere! Add to that five very affectionate (and nosey) kitties and an open plan home and you will begin to understand that sitting anywhere quietly for any length of time is a challenge!

I remember sneaking a chair up to our bedroom one summer's evening, to attempt my daily dose of enlightenment, and as our bedroom door would not shut properly, jamming a doorstop under it from the inside to stop any humans or cats getting in.

I closed the curtains, settled myself down, took a few deep breaths to begin the calming process and then jumped out of my skin as somebody walked very hard into the bedroom door as they tried to come in! Of course the door wouldn't open, so whoever it was put their shoulder to it to have another go; all that did was jam the doorstop further in, so then they started shouting downstairs for me to come up as there was something stopping the door from opening! I leapt up and told them I was trying to meditate, so please go away... AND LEAVE ME IN PEACE!!!

After I had been convinced that it was urgent that they come in and I had given them a bath towel (sigh), I told them to tell everyone else to leave me alone for at least half an hour... Back to the deep breathing with eyes closed to shut out the after image of the bright blue bath towel... and then I screamed out loud as one of the cats leapt up onto my lap having come in from the window!

Chuck out indignant cat, close window, sit down, close eyes, deep breathing... and then son number one put on something very loud from the thrash metal genre in his bedroom. Deep sigh and give up. Go wearily downstairs and flop onto sofa in front of the telly. Surprised (and annoyingly relaxed) husband looks up from the sports pages and asks if I had finished already? Resist the temptation to resort to decidedly un-serene violence!

If your house is anything like mine (and it doesn't get any easier as the kids get older, the noises and questions change, but that's about it!), then you really need to read this!

What is Meditation?

The dictionary defines meditation as:

1.   To engage in thought or contemplation; reflect.

2. To engage in transcendental meditation. Devout religious contemplation, or quiescent spiritual introspection.
3. To consider as something to be done or effected; intend; purpose: to meditate revenge.

I think I should point out that while I cannot recommend that you sit and contemplate just what you intend to wreak on your perceived enemies, it does make a useful point. I shall come back to this in the chapter on the Cosmic Superstore – getting what you want through positive thought.

The Truth about Meditation

Let's get something straight about meditation – as previously mentioned, it does not have to entail sitting in an uncomfortable (or impossible) position for long periods of time, preferably on a mountaintop wearing only a loincloth! Effective meditative states can be achieved in a relatively short length of time – but it is not a competition either!

If you are one of the many people who feel that they can't 'do' meditation because… well, they just can't… then here are the basics to help you minimize this – and give you some strategies to counter it.

Why bother with meditating?

At the time of writing this, I am 51 years old. I have been developing my spiritual self for around 46 of those years, but it is only in the last 13 years that I have understood the need for meditation – and actually been able to get somewhere with it. When I was a teenager, with all the usual emotional angst and hormones hurtling around my system, I read a book on meditation that sounded fabulous in principle… and proved to be impossible in practice. Sadly, I don't have a copy of this book any more; it vanished into the ether somewhere in a house move and I cannot remember the title or author, but to be honest, they are irrelevant.

There are shelves full of books on spiritual development out there like that one.

You buy it because it promises the earth, the stars and all of heaven; you eagerly begin on the first page of Chapter 1, and by the end of the third page, far from feeling that you are on the verge of some deep spiritual truth which will change your life forever, instead you have lost the will to live.

Don't get me wrong, these books have a place; but for the most part they are not for me, or you either, if you are enjoying this book! I wanted something that would give me clear instructions on how to meditate effectively in a way that would enable me to fly with the angels, see, feel and hear God, and touch the stars for good measure.

I don't believe there is a book in all of creation that can do that now, although it would be truly fabulous if it existed; I imagine it would be a bit like a recipe book with God as Jamie Oliver! It would be called 15 Minute Enlightenment and include dozens of easy to put together recipes from an amuse-bouche on how to see ghosts to an elaborate dinner party for your Guides, Guardians and Angels!

However, let's come back to reality here; all forms of spiritual development are a process: whether you just want to know God in a personal way, or become a healer or teacher. There is no one right way of going about it and there is certainly no way of starting from a point of no knowledge to becoming an ascended master in two weeks. It is a lifetime's work, but the rewards are out of this world...

So let's start right at the beginning with meditation and look at why we bother with it at all!

It helps us to find that 'Inner Space' in which we can connect to not only other dimensions – angels, spirits, guides and guardians, but also to that deep core which is our true self. I shall discuss this 'Inner Space' in more depth later, for now just think of it as a sort of internal room in which you can meet folks from other places – an astral social networking site if you like!

It is the most effective method of encouraging that 'shift' in our perceptions of the world: by which I mean being able to extend our senses to see, hear, feel, touch, smell, taste, sense and KNOW things that are not immediately obvious in the physical world.

If you are planning on using your connection for any form of Spiritual Healing, then it is essential you are able to shift your consciousness; meditation will help you to install the internal 'software' that enables you to be able to do this. In fact remembering that the brain is a computer that can be programmed will help you to understand and install any of the processes here. The human brain is the most complex structure so far discovered in the universe. We currently only use a very small proportion of it – think what you could achieve if you could get it working properly!

Meditation has all sorts of add-on bonuses that can improve your life in the physical world… for example a more relaxed state of mind and being, better sleep, the ability to become more focused and determined to succeed, not to mention the potential results of all these things – actually being richer, happier and more successful – I think that is enough to be going on with!

Science has now proved that meditation works on the brain in a physical sense, altering our brain wave patterns, increasing our Alpha Waves which bring about a relaxed state and can help to positively combat anxiety, stress and depression. In fact recent studies have shown that meditating for just ten minutes can have a dramatic effect. It can help us to feel more in control, energized and confident. If we move away from the realms of science and into the domain of spirit, faith and psychic connections, meditation may help us to reach both inwards to our intuition, our inner guidance, and outwards, to the realms of spirit and the angels. By using this tool regularly it may enable us to be able to switch our brains into 'meditation mode' quite quickly, which can be very useful!

What stops us then – if it is so good for us?

This list is compiled from all the reasons I have been given over many years on why meditation is just *not* going to work:

I don't have time
My mind keeps wandering
I cannot 'do' visualization
I fall asleep
I am too restless
I am scared of what I might see
There is nowhere quiet/private for me to meditate
I don't understand it
I haven't tried it but I know it won't work
I have tried it and it doesn't work
It's boring

There are lots more, but these are a selection; the most common by far are the first and last – either *'I don't have time'* or *'I have tried it and it doesn't work'*. What we are going to do now is examine the reasons why meditation is effective and then break down those barriers, one by one.

Breaking Down the Barriers to Meditation

I don't have time! Like you, I have a very busy life and while I would love to have the luxury of being able to meditate for two hours a day, we all know that it is just not going to happen! However, we can find the odd few minutes here and there – for example during coffee and lunch breaks, while keeping an eye on the kids at the park, before going to bed, in the shower… or even while doing the washing up!

I call using these short gaps to daydream your way into a positive form of thinking 'Active Meditation'. I shall discuss this later; it is a very effective method which put simply means that you keep your body busy on a routine task that does not require you to think, and let your mind roam free! Walking, housework, gardening, showering or drying your hair are all great opportunities to spend ten minutes in active meditation. Do NOT attempt to meditate while driving, or operating machinery which requires your full attention!

My mind keeps wandering! Don't worry; this happens to everyone, no matter how 'serene' they may be! We each have what some call the 'Ego Mind': that is your main conscious mind; the part that chatters away inside your head about all the things you should be doing rather than sitting down and spending some 'Me' time. If you suddenly find yourself wondering if the washing machine has finished and needs emptying, then acknowledge the thought and put it to one side and resume your meditation.

It will happen, there is no getting away from it, but by accepting that it will and not stressing over it, it loses the power to disrupt you and, over time, you will find that it happens less and less. By keeping your meditations short, you minimize the chances of your 'Ego Mind' cutting in as frequently.

You might also like to use tools or props to help you; by focusing your eyes upon a candle flame or a crystal for example you may find that it increases your ability to focus.

I cannot 'do' visualization – A great deal of emphasis is placed on visualization in guided meditations; this is where you imagine you are in a particular situation or scenario and use visualization to see how that situation progresses; for example, you might imagine you are walking through a wood and in your mind, you play the scene forward… you have no idea of what will happen, where you end up, who you might meet etc., but there are lessons to be learned from the experience.

In its simplest form, visualization is nothing more than daydreaming – and this is a skill that all of us possess. I used to while away Latin lessons at school by staring out of the window and dreaming of what I would say to the Bay City Rollers (Scottish teen pop group whose screaming pubescent fans coined the phrase 'Rollermania' in the 1970's) in the unlikely event that I ever met them (I didn't)… later on the picture changed with my music tastes and it was Freddie Mercury in my dreams; these days it is more likely to be the Bank Manager, although he (or she) is almost as mythical in my mind as the pop stars I lusted after in the 1970s!

We have all 'practiced' a conversation in our head; the interview for the job we desperately want, the casual but devastatingly insightful chat with the person you fancy… if you ever pluck up the courage to speak to them at all of course… and then there are the truly difficult moments in life, telling someone we no longer want to be with them, that a loved one has died, that you have been diagnosed with cancer… we all have a picture in our mind of how these scenarios will play out; we practice them over and over to cover our responses to any questions that might come up, to cope with what might happen.

Visualization during meditation works on exactly the same principle as this: you are using it as a tool to connect you to another part of your mind, another realm; to see who pops up along the way, what places you visit and what decisions and actions you take. You can also note any sounds you hear, or how you feel during the visualization.

Exercise – To test your own visualization skills, try visualizing yourself doing something routine, such as travelling to work, or taking the children to school. Run through the whole procedure in your mind, from putting on your coat, to leaving the house, the details of your journey and your arrival at your destination.

I fall asleep – I try not to meditate in bed for just this reason. Falling asleep while in a meditation is fairly common; the combination of being warm and relaxed with slowing your brain waves is just too comfortable! The key to this is not to meditate lying down; sit in a straight-backed, but comfortable chair – and of course, by using a short meditation routine, there is less time to get that relaxed! However, there are occasions when meditation in bed is exactly what I do need; when I cannot sleep for example, I have a short routine that is guaranteed to bring me into the gentle realm of sleep… I'll share it with you later.

I am too restless – This can take several forms, from the overactive mind kicking in all the time, to feeling 'twitchy' on your seat and unable to keep still. Since I entered the menopause, I have found that sitting or standing completely still for any length of time is frankly impossible; I get a sort of tingly feeling in my arms and legs and start to feel agitated if I can't walk around! I cannot make up my mind as to whether this is a genuine side effect of being menopausal or just me…

Minimize the problem by first of all ensuring that the chair is comfortable and your feet are flat on the ground. Meditation always starts with a few deep and slow breaths; try adding a couple more in to boost your oxygen levels. This has the effect of making you more alert and calm.

It is also worth remembering that if you have something particular on your mind, something important, then you are probably not going to be able to achieve much meditating. I can remember many years ago when I was waiting to see if the offer we had made on a house was going to be accepted; my attempt to shut down my overactive mind came down to one phrase being repeated over and over in my head... 'Please say yes, please say yes, please say yes!' They said yes.

Many people suffer from physical restlessness that can get in the way of their efforts to meditate; from not knowing what to do with their hands, to restless legs and feet that insist on drumming a beat out on the floor. You may find that **'Active Meditation'**, mentioned previously, may be easier for you. Oh and did I mention? Don't meditate for too long!

I am scared of what I might see – This one also includes the 'Spawn of the Devil' issue...!

Some people are concerned that opening themselves up to spiritual development may let in all sorts of undesirable elements which in the worst case scenario might mean they end up with their head spinning round and their skin turning green while projectile vomiting over priests! It also covers those who may have experienced something, perhaps at an early age, which alarmed or frightened them and made them close down.

Children are much more open to the spiritual side of life; they have not yet had time to acquire the prejudices and fears of adults. This is fantastic when it comes to seeing fairies at the bottom of the garden, but perhaps less so when they come screaming into your bed at night complaining that there is a monster in their wardrobe! As parents, we tend to deal with both of these scenarios in a similar way – by telling the child that the fairies and monsters don't exist, which is a pity, because we are helping them to shut down not just their spiritual connections, but their imagination. How would you react if your child had an 'imaginary' friend? Tell them it was a figment of their imagi-nation – or ask them to describe the friend and not be dismissive. If we are dismissive of our child's fears, those fears won't go away, they'll just hide them. I know this from my own experience; I felt threatened by a ghostly female figure in my childhood home. I tried talking about her, but it was dismissed.

On one occasion, Little Grandma was babysitting and I dreamt I was being throttled by this woman; I awoke to discover I was throwing up onto the pillow. Grandma would not listen to my fears, she was angry that she had to change my bedding and determined that I should go back to sleep in the same room – even though I was plainly terrified. This dream, or vision, call it what you will, was so vivid that I can remember every detail of it even now, some 42 years later. I can even remember the color of the sunset, and how the vivid golden sky made me feel somehow threatened.

I believe that rather than being dismissive, we need to listen to what our children say; if they feel threatened, we need to give them a means of defense, if they see something beautiful and ethereal, we should ask them to describe it, draw a picture, let us into that experience – not tell them it is all rubbish.

When that child grows up, think how much easier it will be to enhance their connection to spirit if they are not having to peel away the layers of parental disapproval... of having to build in layers of belief once more. My feeling is that children should be allowed to develop their beliefs and connections naturally, parents are there to guide – and of course you will want to talk to your child about your faith or religion; but if at a later stage they decide on a different path to ours, we should not be offended.

It is important to realize that **you** *are in control of your development; it is not in control of you.*

If you see or experience things which make you anxious, then ask your guides, guardians and angels to slow down the pace, or take that experience away from you for the time being. You can always open up to it again later, when you feel ready.

The 'Spawn of the Devil' issue.

Over the years I have worked in many aspects of the Mind, Body and Spirit industry. I have made stuff, written stuff, painted stuff, performed readings and healing... all with the highest and best interests, all with only good in my heart and my soul. Sadly, however, there are still folks out there who cannot quite get to grips with this sort of thing. Thankfully, there are no villagers out there with burning brands and pitchforks (hopefully) any more! The worst we experienced was being banned from a parish council controlled venue for, presumably, being in league with the devil.

There is nowhere quiet/private for me to meditate – This is another reason for using short periods of time that may be easier to manage. However, if there really is nowhere that you will feel comfortable, or if you want to carry your space with you, then **'Active Meditation'** mentioned earlier is an option. You may have to be creative in choosing when and where you meditate. I could give you a long list of all the places that are unsuitable for peace and quiet, but I'm not going to. Unless you are very, very lucky, it probably includes your home, most of the time… Look for the short spaces, the niches in your day in which you can find a few minutes…

I don't understand it – Some people have what I like to call a 'scientific mind' which likes to see concrete proof before they will try anything, or believe in anything. As mentioned before, meditation has been scientifically proven to be beneficial; there are lots of resources to help you understand the rational elements behind this ancient practice. All you need is an Internet connection and a search engine. Just type in the following phrase: 'What is the evidence that meditation is effective'.

I have found that for some this statement hides a deeper question, which may relate to issues of anxiety; you may need to assess how you react to trying new things in general – it may fall under that heading of 'I am scared'. For others it may be that they have previously not considered meditation or spiritual development and just need to find out more.

I have not tried it but I know it won't work – As your mum no doubt said when you were small and faced with something new on your plate at dinnertime… "If you don't try it how do you know you won't like it?"

We have to be willing to *try*; if you genuinely want to develop your spirituality, you have to be prepared to open your mind to the possibilities and many benefits that meditation has to offer. In fact a closed mind is one of the biggest barriers to development, because after all, that is what spiritual development is all about, opening your mind. When you do try it (if you do), then be wholehearted about your approach; if you go into it thinking, 'This won't work', then it probably won't.

I have tried it and it didn't work – This is very common and what you need to do is to – *honestly* – review the experience you previously had.

How many times did you attempt it?

Were you being honest and wholehearted about your approach?

Have you tried different methods?

After all, not everyone is the same and there are many methods of meditating. It may be that the one you chose was not suitable for your temperament or lifestyle. Does the reason it did not succeed on that occasion fall into one of the categories listed here?

Are you really being honest about your efforts – or have you decided somewhere inside that, as this will really not work for you, there is no point in trying anyway.

An open heart and a positive approach will yield the best results. No ifs or buts!

If you are bloody-minded about trying, then it simply will not get you anywhere, and who are you trying to fool? This is something that only *you* can experience, or measure the success or failure of.

I suffer from being bloody-minded – just ask my husband. However, I am also not afraid of admitting when I am wrong – sometimes, on very rare occasions when there are two moons in the sky! If I want something badly enough, I will keep trying until I succeed, or have to admit that I have tried, done my best and it is not for me. We had swimming lessons at school; the instructor proudly told us that no child had ever left the school without being able to swim. They failed with me… I had nearly drowned a few years previously on a family holiday in Cornwall; I was terrified of tripping and falling under the water and as a result developed a phobia of water falling onto my face. It was so bad I would not even take a shower – baths all the way for me – until I was 40. My 40th birthday present to myself was to learn to swim. My best friend (as bad as me) and I joined a class at the local pool called 'Adult Swimming for the Terrified'… (yes, really!); within a month I was walking on my hands on the bottom of the pool and wondering why on earth I had not learned earlier! I love the sensation of being supported by the water; it turns out that I do not inevitably sink to the bottom after all; actually I seem to have more than my fair share of personal buoyancy aids and find it tricky to stay underwater without floating up to the surface! If you had told me all those years ago that one day I would be told off for not being able to sit on the bottom of the pool, I would have laughed at you.

There are two points here. The first is that it needs to be the right time for you; if you are not ready to honestly – and with an open heart and mind – commit yourself fully to the task in hand, it ain't gonna work. The second is to find the right teacher; my school instructor used blunt bullying methods, something which only succeeded in putting my back up and making me deter-mined to prove her wrong. The instructor on the course at my local pool was firm and confident in her belief that anyone could learn to swim, but was willing to listen to our fears, and gentle in her approach. The group was small too, which meant that none of us at any time felt threatened; we did not feel overwhelmed by the numbers of other students, and we were confident that if we did get into trouble, she would be able to get to us quickly.

Like that second teacher, I am confident that everyone can succeed in developing a spiritual life; I also understand that it is a different experience for each individual. In addition to this I know that we each have limitations… in the same way that Usain Bolt has the gift of hurtling along at an unbelievable pace for one human being, but I can barely hobble to the bathroom in the morning.

Each of us starts at the beginning. Each of us makes the journey. Each of us stops at a different point. Some of us choose to continue on the journey forever.

It's boring – Saying something is boring often hides something else… It might be one of the things I have already mentioned, or it might be something else. It might just be that you have not yet found the key that unlocks your mind and sparks your imagination; much of what happens on your spiritual path will come from within, so finding a key to unlock your door to imagination is essential. I see my spiritual journey as walking through a forest on the edge of a sea; you might see yours as journeying through Middle Earth, or within the pages of a Manga novel; really the choice is up to you and nobody else, because nobody else can see it. You are free to be who you want to be, and it is so much better than *Second Life*, or *Halo* or any of the other online virtual reality scenarios, because YOU are in charge, you are not following someone else's programmed dance.

In Summary – Whatever your feelings about meditation, it is the best method – most tried and tested – of actually getting some positive results from your development path.

It need not be a chore – something that has to be done under sufferance; there are many ways of making it a more appealing task not the least of which are those beneficial results!

Try to build it into your day; shorter lengths of time, on the 'little and often' principle, will help to speed things along more (in my opinion); take those ten minute opportunities – waiting for the washing machine to finish; for the kids to finally be ready; between your favorite programs – look for the gaps, no matter how small.

Once you are familiar with the basics you may feel that you want to embark on a longer internal journey – there are some ideas at the end in the exercise chapter.

Remember to keep a diary of your progress and experiences while in meditation; you may find that others have similar experiences which you can discuss – and you will find that you can look back and see how fast you moved along your path!

If, after reading all this, you are still not convinced, then try writing a For and Against list to understand your true feelings; you have to be honest with yourself, nobody else will see it, and if you cannot be honest with yourself...?

FOR – Reasons why I want to... AGAINST – Reasons why I don't want to, or cannot see the point...

Preparing for Meditation

You want to give yourself the best possible chance of getting results from your efforts and a little thought beforehand will help to maximize this. As your skill and experience grows, you will find that you can 'click in' to the mindset at any time, but you may still find it useful to follow the following guidelines for deeper or more important meditations.

There are three main things to consider: Yourself. Your environment. Any tools or props to assist your focus.

Yourself – It is always worth considering your own comfort, even for a ten minute meditation!

Tight clothing, recent large meals or alcohol consumption are not ideal; try and be as comfortable as possible, given the environment you intend spending time in and ensuring you start with a clear mind.

If meditating while sitting still, use a straight-backed chair, feet firmly planted on the ground, hands resting lightly on your lap, with the palms uppermost. It may seem a little picky, but your posture really is vital. If you sit slouched, your spine will hurt fairly rapidly, if your feet are not comfortably placed, your legs begin to ache and that quickly sets your spine jangling... If you cannot find a chair in which you reach the ground with your feet comfortably, then find a book to put under them, if they need bringing up... or to put on the seat of the chair to bring them down...

Don't bother trying to hold your stomach in. Really, don't.

Your Environment – Now this can be anywhere from your home to a forest glade, the shore of a lake or the sea, your car, or even your workplace.

At home, you might want to close the curtains, or dim the lights, make sure you have a suitable chair on which you can sit comfortably, with your feet flat upon the ground. Remember, are your legs comfortable? If not, then place a large book or something similar under your feet and see if that makes a difference!

If you have difficulty in sitting, then lay down, but I only recommend this if you really do have trouble sitting as we want a good, strong and positive flow of energy, from your feet upwards. If you are lying down, the energy may not flow as well. (There are a couple of exercises which I have specifically written to be carried out while lying down.)

When you are outside, and able to sit down, then try and select somewhere dry at least! (Or bring a waterproof cushion...)

You also might want to have some water nearby as a drink after meditating can help to bring you back properly and ground you.

If you are engaged on an active meditation, then all you need is to focus your automatic actions on whatever you are physically doing, while freeing the subconscious mind to meditate.

I do need to repeat that you must *not* try to meditate while doing something that requires your full attention, such as driving.

Tools or props to assist your focus – There are various things which can help to create the sort of atmosphere that may help you to program your brain into expecting meditation. These are of course individual to each of us, but may include the following:

Candle flame
Crystal
Mandala (usually geometric patterns)
Abstract Painting
Music

Whatever you decide to use remember that you want this to help you to focus on keeping your mind clear of distractions; for example, if you use music, I recommend something instrumental and not too loud or your mind will start to hook onto the lyrics and before you know it you are singing along in your mind and not concentrating on your meditation!

If you use a visual tool, such as a crystal or candle flame, then allow your eyes to become unfocused slightly and just gaze within the object.

Putting a clear crystal onto a light box with a *slowly* rotating color change system is very good; it allows your ego mind to take note of all the internal twists and turns within the crystal and keeps it happy, while your higher mind concentrates on the matter in hand. I have one light box which rotates the colors so fast, it reminds me of a glitter ball – I have a beautiful glass angel who lives on it, I call her my disco angel!

In summary – Whatever methods you use to help you find a way to meditate, or be mindful – the important thing is to try… it need not be difficult, time consuming or complicated… and the benefits are many. If, like me, you really struggle with the whole sitting down quietly bit, my personal solution will definitely work for you.

Active Meditation

Active Meditation was born out of my struggle to find peace and quiet; I tried everything, from getting up early (me?!) to staying up late, which just made me feel resentful that everyone else was in bed and I wasn't. I tried telling the family to be quiet and leave me alone – which made them resentful – and I even tried sitting in my car. That particular exercise nearly led to an ambulance being called out for me; a passerby thought I might be having a heart attack! I tried so many different things and in the end I realized that it was hopeless to try and fit my life around the meditation, **I had to make the meditation fit into my life!**

There are three very simple, utterly foolproof steps to getting somewhere with meditation:

1. Junk the word 'Meditation'
2. Open your heart and mind
3. Actually do it

That's it. Let's look at this in a bit more depth.

Junk the word 'Meditation'

When you were a kid, how did you feel when your teachers told you that you had to do your homework? If you tell me that you accepted it gratefully and with a happy heart every single time, I'm sorry, but I won't believe you! Each one of us has a rebellious child lurking within; they never go away, no matter how old we are. When we are told to do something that we don't fancy much, or which might be hard work, or seen as boring, repetitive and pointless – because it won't work anyway – then we are going to dredge up every teeny tiny reason for not even starting.

Here's a personal example; I'm not proud of this, by the way, but it illustrates the point beautifully. When I was in my final year at school, I had loads of homework, as you would expect. I spent time on the English, Art, History... all the subjects I loved, but when it came to science, well, just yuck! I had to do science, it was compulsory, but that didn't mean I had to like it; sound familiar? I was doing a combined Physics and Chemistry exam (they were called 'O Levels' in England in the 1970's), and while the Physics part was OK, I took a real dislike to the Chemistry, partly because I couldn't understand most of it. In that final year, I didn't hand in any chemistry homework; in fact, I didn't even get as far as writing my name on the front of the book! Like I say, I'm not proud of this, and I hope that these days, the teacher might even get as far as trying to help me. I used to be blessed with a virtually photographic memory and somehow scraped through the exam with a C grade; it wouldn't happen now, I'm lucky to be able to remember what I had for dinner last night!

Here's a different example, to show how it doesn't matter how old you are, that rebellious child is still in there stamping her tiny feet!

My grandma was an amazing woman; born in 1918, she worked immensely hard all her life and passed away in April 2012, at the age of 93. Her garden was her pride and joy; she worked on the same plot of land for almost 60 years, and in the summer it was filled with light and color. She told me a few weeks before she passed that the happiest days of her life were spent in her garden.

A few years before she died, she broke her hip. She was moving a heavy plant pot but the ancient plastic tub had become brittle and it disintegrated as she lifted it, which threw her off balance and she fell awkwardly. The doctors pinned her back together and after a short stay in the hospital, she came home, armed with a pair of crutches. The doctor was most insistent that she must use the crutches and there was to be absolutely no gardening until she was given the all clear…

No gardening? Walk with stupid crutches? They didn't have a prayer… my grandma's inner rebellious child reared up and although Mum and I did our best, she just went back to doing what she damn well wanted to! No matter that it would help her recover more quickly, or more completely, she was not going to behave and that was that. Mum took her back for a case review with her consultant some months after the incident; as they entered the consultation room, the doctor boomed out: "Mrs. Coleman, why are you not using your crutches! Your hip is held together with metal pins, until it's fully healed; it could give way at any moment!"

Grandma fixed him with a hard stare and said something very rude… Mum thought she had better not tell him that Grandma had been digging over the garden the previous day…

A couple of weeks (and much nagging) later, Mum and I took her into town, having persuaded her to take the hated crutches with her… She put her arms into them, and trailed them behind her like a sulky child, as a trip hazard for anyone unlucky enough to be near. Rebellious child? Grandma wrote the book!

The point of all this is that it is absolutely vital that YOU want to do this; if anyone says you *must* do something, or *should* be doing something, it won't work. It has to come from you.

I can give you some ideas on alternative words, but to be honest, it's best if it comes from you, that it's your own idea. That way, you will be more committed to it. Once it becomes natural for you, a part of your life, you won't need words, it just is.

Open your heart and mind

That sounds nice and simple, and it is – but you do actually have to do it! Be open to the possibilities… you don't want that rebellious child to stamp her pretty foot. If you have already made up your mind that it won't work, then it won't work.

We all know that a negative outlook or attitude can block your progress... but that doesn't stop us from doing it sometimes. Think of a time at work, for example, when a new system or way of doing things has been introduced; we can be very resistant to change, especially if perhaps it has been brought in by someone new, someone who doesn't understand that this is the way it has always been done. In the modern working world, we all have to be flexible; a company that can't or won't adapt to fit the economic climate and trends and evolve may not survive.

Where your spiritual self is concerned, how you develop and what success you have can be really affected by your willingness to be open. OK, so maybe sitting in a loincloth is either not working or is completely impractical for you; that does not mean that all forms of meditation (or whatever you choose to call it) therefore won't work either.

So what do you think about?

You've made yourself comfy, gone out for a walk or whatever works for you... now all you have to do is decide what to meditate on. I've meditated on anything from meeting guides, guardians and angels, to visualizing a successful shopping trip, especially at Christmas! Let me give you an example.

I used to have nightmares about forgetting someone at Christmas; I would dream that I was in the local gift shop, on Christmas Eve, just as the shop was closing. I would be panicking because right at the last moment, I had remembered that I had no gift for someone really important... my mum, or stepdad, or my best friend. I would rush around the shop, looking frantically at shelves either emptied by other, more fortunate shoppers, or with only a couple of random items left on them, the sort of things nobody in their right mind would either buy, or want as a gift. On one mind-boggling occasion, I bought a half-eaten pasty and a necklace made of clothes pegs strung onto a tatty shoelace for Mum in one of these nocturnal visits. Of course I knew that the dreams were brought about by my anxiety over finding the right gifts, in good time, at the right prices, but it's no good knowing what the problem is, unless you have a solution – and back then, I was so utterly rubbish at organizing my life, that there was a good chance of somebody being horrified when they unwrapped a half-eaten pasty on Christmas morning.

After a mere 15 years of being stuck in the Christmas shopping nightmare, I discovered the solution, and it was meditation. Nothing formal, no sitting in a semi-darkened room, just an acknowledgement that taking action early would sort it out. Sometime around the end of October, I will meditate on Christmas Shopping, as I do my household chores, sorting out the washing, cleaning the bathroom. I visualize the joy on Christmas morning as the gifts are opened, and then work it back, like running a film backwards, through the wrapping process, looking at the gifts, as I wrap them, back to storing them in my wardrobe (it's alright, the kids already know where Father Christmas hides the presents), to the actual shopping process. Of course I ask people what they would like, and of course I check prices and search the net and all those sorts of things, but visualizing my trip to the shops means that when the time comes, I know what I am looking for, am less likely to be distracted by stuff I cannot afford and feel calmer about the whole process. Once I took action to make sure the nightmare would not become a reality, it faded away.

Visualization is an incredibly powerful tool; all successful athletes use it to play out the process of their competitions so that they are ready to cope with whatever happens on the day. I have used it to help me shop, slim, drive long distances without getting lost (always a challenge for me) and succeed when applying for jobs. It's nothing 'weirdy' or 'out there'; it's an accepted and effective method of achieving something. It's especially good when you need to stay calm in a stressful situation, from exams and tests, to interviews, sitting in the dentist's chair and even for your wedding day. Playing out the process in your mind, over and over again, so that every stage becomes very familiar, means that when the actual situation arises, you know what to do, because you've been there already, over and over and over again. Remember, the more you practice the visualization, the more effective it is.

If you can't think of anything to meditate on, or you want a specific focus, then Guided Meditation can help. There are some free downloads on my website at: michellejones.me.uk. Guided Meditation means that you listen to someone speaking, guiding you along a predetermined path. It might be on a CD or download, or might be performed live at a workshop. I like guided meditation for various reasons; it's useful when you really want to stay focused on a particular theme, or are working towards a specific result and can be carried through from start to finish, or may lead you part of the way along the path before leaving you to carry on yourself.

Sometimes you may not get the desired result on the first attempt, but it's worth the effort to keep going as the repetition is gently effective. Let me give you an example.

I had a difficult relationship with my father. He was a controlling man who was a nightmare to live with when I was growing up; he was very miserly with my mother and me and my brothers, and had one phase of not speaking to any of us which lasted more than two years. Some years ago, I did a course of workshops to help me work on how I felt about him, and to forgive him. One guided meditation involved rowing across a beautiful lake; I had to glide serenely across the silver water thinking nice thoughts until I became aware of the sounds of someone struggling in the water. I rowed across to the source of the sound and discovered my father trying and failing to swim;

I then had to grab hold of him, pull him out of the water and row him to safety – this would begin the forgiveness process.

In my case, I rowed across the water, rowed over to Dad, hoisted him unceremoniously over the edge of the boat and watched him gasping like a fish on the wooden planks of the hull for about five minutes, before chucking him back in and rowing off to the nearest pub. I don't think I was quite ready to forgive right then! I have forgiven him now, but that method was not right for me, for that situation. What helped me in the end was understanding that you can forgive the person, but perhaps not the actions. It enables you to be able to deal with that person on a day to day basis, without feeling that there is always an elephant in the room.

I've talked about using those small spaces in your day to carry your spiritual self and development around with you, but there is one space in the day that each and every one of us has. This is the space between getting into our bed and falling asleep. There are some who feel that any form of meditation or spiritual work done while in bed is a 'bad thing' because we may fall asleep, but nothing 'bad' can happen if you fall asleep while meditating, and I use it sometimes for that very reason, to help me sleep.

I use the time when attempting to fall asleep to set myself up for the night ahead, to try and feel my way forwards into my dreams. Now as I have some pretty peculiar dreams it's probably for you to decide how successful I really am… but sometimes, I have some incredibly powerful and profound dreams that I know are a result of tapping into some greater force…

One of the things I love about dreams is that they can be used as a meeting place, for the dreamer to have conversations with people who might otherwise be out of reach, for one reason or another. I have a recurring dream in which I meet Robbie Williams in a stairwell.

I appreciate that this sounds a bit weird to start with, but for me there is a point to it. Each time that we meet, it is at a different point on the stairs, at a higher, or lower level. The stairwell is a square one, echoey, the sort you might find in a tall building. It's always very clean, so we're not talking derelict skyscraper or tower block, it's bright and clean... and empty. We never see anyone else on the stairs.

This dream has popped up half a dozen times in the last 15 years or so; it's difficult to say whether it is a 'genuine' spiritual meeting, or just a dream – I guess I shall never find out unless I meet Robbie one day and discover that he has been dreaming about meeting a mysterious mad woman in a lonely stairwell!

The dream always develops in the same way; I am in a very old house with dark wood paneling, and discover a hidden door behind a red velvet curtain. I walk through the door and find myself in the stairwell. Robbie will either come up, or down the stairs and stop to talk; our conversations are always about how he feels about himself. I try to reassure him. You can argue that all of this just comes up because I want him to be happy and successful – which I do – but it feels to me as though there is a much deeper level to it too. The stairwell could represent where we are on our spiritual journey: when we feel disconnected and anxious, we move down a level; when we have one of those rare but wonderful days when everything feels in tune, we move up a level.

My Robbie dreams always end with him climbing the stairs to the next landing, and me leaving through same the door back into the dark house with the wood paneling.

You can use your dreams as a meditation space with a technique called Lucid Dreaming. It can be as complicated or as simple as you like, but it boils down to knowing in the dream that you are dreaming, and then being able to direct the dream in any way that you fancy. I think I'd steer clear of fantasies involving celebs though... Lucid dreaming requires lots of practice and an acceptance that you are almost certainly going to fail at first, but everyone can succeed at using their dreams to communicate with their angels. I'll talk more about that in a later chapter.

The truth about meditation is that without it, or some form of it, you are going to find connecting to an internal spiritual life almost impossible, but it does not have to be difficult. Use daydreams, use the time when cleaning your teeth, waiting in the queue at the bank, walking to your car, working out at the gym, swimming, showering – use every minute you can to just tune in to your inner life and it will absolutely work. Bin the loincloth for good!

Chapter 4

Keeping Your Feet on the Ground

Don't let go of your kite strings!

I spent years trying to raise the level of my consciousness – or 'get out of my head' if you prefer – to absolutely no good effect. I would like to reassure you that no illegal substances were used, although I did go through a few tubes of 'Deep Heat' for my aching muscles. Hours and hours of sitting around feeling hideously uncomfortable in the dark hoping that at some point I was going to be somehow transcended into a wonderful new realm, preferably populated with angels and ascended masters.

But nothing. Zilch. All I achieved was backache and a sore bum!

There were many reasons for my lack of success, which I am going to solve for you in this book, so that you don't make the same mistakes I did – but one of those reasons was so glaringly obvious that I completely missed it for years. Let me explain.

We love going out to fly our kites. When the kids were little we bought colorful 'Thomas the Tank Engine' kites and pocket kites – incidentally, those pocket kites are absolutely brilliant as a marker for your spot on a busy field or beach. They stay up without any effort and you can tie them to your windbreak or chair. Then, when you have wandered off for an ice cream it makes it really easy to see where you are headed back to. If you've got kids wandering around, it makes it a lot easier for them too, and gives you a bit of extra peace of mind. I'm digressing again! As the children grew older, they weren't satisfied with a kite that just 'stayed up', and we moved on to stunt kites that swooped and dived across the sky. Then, one day, we saw a man on the Isle of Wight flying a power kite.

We were transfixed. The kite had four lines attached to straps secured to his forearms and we could see the muscles standing out as he controlled it in the stiff wind. Every now and again he would run and jump with it, incredibly long and high jumps that reminded me of the seven-league boots of European folklore. It looked really dangerous – and utterly brilliant!

That was the start of an expensive love affair with power kites, that still continues now. We started with the smallest one; took it up to the summit of Butser Hill on the South Downs and carefully attached the lines. It didn't feel that windy up there but as Phil released it, it shot off into the sky like a guided missile and immediately pulled me over, dragging me along the ground! Phil helped me up, concerned for my welfare, but I could see he was desperate to have a go himself, so I let him remove the Velcro straps connecting me to the lines and put them on himself. I cast the smallest power kite available to buy into the blue sky again. My husband is not a small chap; he stands six feet tall, is broad shouldered and strong, but it easily defeated his ability to control it. In one of those moments that will stay with you forever, I stood and watched as he ran crazily across the hilltop in zigzags completely at the mercy of the little kite and the wind. I could hear the music from *The Benny Hill Show* playing in my head as Phil rapidly lurched staggering from side to side; his shorts were starting to fall down now and I could see it was only going to end in one way. There was a particularly strong gust of wind and Phil was pulled clean off his feet, landing heavily on the grass, arms still held aloft as the malicious kite tried to add insult to injury by pulling him inexorably along the ground towards a big juicy cowpat. I ran over to him, barely able to breathe for laughing. Phil was barely able to breathe as well, winded by the impact, but he was trying to laugh too!

We have moved on now to much bigger kites several meters across, but we have also learned that you don't launch them straight into the wind! You take a sideways approach, sending them skywards on the edges of the 'wind window' which allows you to control the kite, rather than the kite controlling you. It's an amazing feeling to be out early on a deserted beach at any time; add in a power kite and it's a recipe for pure exhilaration!

Spiritual development can be a lot like learning to fly a kite. It's no good trying to fly a 5 meter monster, unless you've learned to control the little ones first! If you go out to fly a kite, before you let it go, make sure you firmly attach the lines; if you are working to raise your consciousness you need to make sure the connection to your body and the real world is firmly attached, so that no matter how high you go, there is a clear path back.

This connection is called grounding and it can be as complicated or as simple as you want it to be. I did a workshop about 15 years ago that included a grounding ritual that took twenty minutes to perform and included tying one of your shoelaces to the leg of the chair on which you were sitting. I was desperate to ask what you did if you were not wearing shoes with laces, as mine were fastened with Velcro, but did not have the courage! They had stipulated that trainers must be worn for comfort, but I suspect that it was more to do with the tying the laces to the leg of the chair thing!

I have a much easier solution: an imaginary extending lead that plugs you in to the earth's core. This is a very special sort of lead; it never ever gets tangled up in anything, unlike every other lead on the planet. It is a very simple idea, a bit like the extending and retracting lead on a vacuum cleaner; you pull out as much as you need, and then with the push of a button, it rewinds neatly at speed.

It works very well; but is most effective if you put a little effort into installing the software properly the first time you use it. "Software?" I hear you say... The brain is a computer; we are all familiar with that as a concept, so it follows then that anything new that we learn – reading, driving, applying mascara – is effectively new software, an App if you like! Over the years I have chosen to install the 'Babies and Childcare' App, the 'Pandering to Finicky Eaters' App and more recently the 'Coping with Teenagers' App, but I have deleted the 'Bedroom Tidying' App. They're on their own with that now.

To install the grounding App into your brain, take a few moments to really think about what you are doing; if you want to sit and use a traditional meditation technique that's fine, but thinking about it while performing a routine task, such as housework, walking or even changing a diaper is equally fine! Whichever method of meditation or mindfulness you use, this is what you need to do.

Grounding App – Plugging in to the Earth

Imagine that there is an electric cable which is wound up inside your feet. It's quite safe, it cannot affect your everyday life in any way, but when you need that grounding connection to be really active, it will spring into action. Watch as it rapidly unwinds, shooting down into the ground, through the floors if you are inside a building, down through the layers of concrete and soil, through the strata of roots and archaeology, down past the bedrock, through millions of years of history... until it reaches the glowing magma at the center of the planet. Now the end of the cable forms into a plug which securely connects to a socket formed in the magma. This connection is completely safe, keeping you grounded and safe, leaving you free to traverse the heavens with your mind.

If you can, think about this slowly the first time you do it, think about each stage of the layers of the earth; it doesn't matter if you get these in the right order, or even if they are the right layers – you could have layers of cream cheese and chocolate – what matters is that you take your time over it. Once you have done this, whenever you need that connection in the future, you can bring it into being at a moment's notice, just like flicking a switch!

There are many other ways of grounding and images you can use; I use the extending lead most of the time for sheer simplicity, but if I want to connect to a particular place then I imagine that roots are growing from my body, spreading out and down. These are both well-known methods but anything that you can relate to which firmly anchors you to the earth is fine.

There are many advantages to this grounding connection; if you feel lethargic or need a boost, you can plug yourself in and visualize earth energy flowing up the cable to energize you; it's amazing how much of a kick this can provide, especially when you are at the end of the day struggling to park in an overcrowded supermarket car park, preparing for the slog around the aisles.

Staying grounded is one of the key skills that motors any form of spiritual training or development forwards. As I said earlier, I struggled for years to succeed with meditation and spiritual development. It is just not enough to sit down in that well-worn loincloth and think of nothing.

So what happens if you do not bother with the whole grounding thing? You are certainly not going to end up with a personality disorder, or possessed by an opportunist demon, just looking for an empty body carelessly left unoccupied by someone meditating – but you might begin to feel seriously 'spaced' and find it difficult to concentrate for a while. We have all experienced days when we complain that we don't feel quite there... or not with it... boosting your grounding connection with a few deep breaths while visualizing your personal extension lead plugging in can have an immediate benefit! What I want to get across here is that this is not just for the rare occasions when you have the time to take time out; making this a part of your everyday life, building it into your day, can have a real and measurable effect.

Think about those times when you really need to be focused: during exams, driving lessons and tests, interviews, presentations, etc. Taking a few moments for a few deep breaths while you ground yourself can help you achieve the concentration you need for the best result.

There are different levels of grounding; the above technique is ideal for any daily situations, but you can achieve a deeper level of grounding by tapping into those places that seem to speak to you, that feel special. These places can help us recharge our spiritual batteries, help us to relax and recover from anxiety and stress, and find the space and clarity needed to think about life's situations.

We all have places which feel special to us; for example when we visit the Chalice Well Gardens in Glastonbury, or our favorite beach in Cornwall, I like to drink in the atmosphere by grounding myself to that specific point. It's different for each place; in Glastonbury I sit quietly on the stone wall by a beautiful waterfall which then runs through a channel in front of me, before draining into a pool. In my mind I carefully move through the grounding process, imagining what those layers might be like immediately below my feet. They will probably be different for each individual that sits on the stone wall, but it doesn't matter, because this is your experience, your vision. For me, the Chalice Well Gardens are a magical place filled with peace and calming, healing energy. On the beach I stand as far away from the shore as possible – and the tide goes out a very long way in the Camel Estuary near Padstow! I stand with my feet in the water, toes plugged into the wet, soft sand and feel that earthing connection in an entirely different way; this is sparkling, energizing and uplifting, especially if the wind is blowing in from the sea on the turn of the tide! Depending on my mood, or what I need at the time, I can use that Grounding App to plug me in to the energy of a specific place without needing to be there, so that when I need peace and healing I can flick the internal switch connecting me to the Chalice Well Gardens, or when I need to feel the energy of the sea, I plug into the beach near Padstow! I have many other special places of course, places that also have different meanings and energy signatures for me: a path, a particular tree, or a view from the A3 main road between London and Portsmouth that means I'm nearly home.

The A3 has played a large part in my life. I was born in Portsmouth, at the southern end and I still live close to the old A3, less than a mile from the modern dual carriageway. I can hear you asking how on earth can a road have an impact on your spiritual well-being!

I have travelled hundreds of thousands of miles up and down the A3, between Portsmouth and Petersfield, over the course of my life. My grandparents bought a house in Portsmouth in 1953, where my parents now live, so I have an incredibly strong connection to the city. I'm also a lifelong fan of Portsmouth 'Pompey' football club (for my sins) and am a season ticket holder. You can't beat the sheer passion, grit and determination of the Pompey fans – and visiting Fratton Park is most definitely a grounding experience!

The kids all attended the preschool and primary school in Buriton, a small village just outside Petersfield. We drove up and down the A3 on school runs for 14 years; we worked out that we must have travelled approximately 120,000 miles just taking the kids to school!

As you travel north from Horndean, you can see Windmill Down on the right; I had been driving up and down the A3 for years before I finally noticed the footpath. It was the white van that I saw first; it was parked just off the main road, presumably in a lay-by. I noticed it because the van was starkly out of place against the fields on the hillside, but I expect the driver had stopped for a tea break. He was back again the following day and the day after that too, but then I presume he had completed whatever brought him to the area, and I never saw the van again. It had performed its purpose though; I had seen the path up the hillside, and was looking at it every day as I drove back and forth. I became aware of a need to walk up that path, but I couldn't work out why I felt so strongly. I did have my own research assistant at home who could help me though; Phil is a self-confessed map addict and immediately dug out all the historical maps of the area he had – it didn't take him long to find out that the spot was called Snell's Corner, although who Snell might have been was, and still is, a complete mystery.

Now of course, we all turn to Google to see what's there, or what might have been there; the Internet was in its infancy back in the mid 1990s, and we had only just gone online. Some of you won't even remember the painful slowness of the net on a dial-up connection or the distinctive sound of the connection process! Remember life before the net; our children cannot imagine how we ever coped! It might have taken a while, but still, one day it occurred to me to search online for archaeological reports of the area and to my astonishment there was information which directly related to Snell's Corner!

In 1947, an archaeological investigation was carried out in advance of widening the London Road (A3) at Horndean. It discovered an ancient burial site at Snell's Corner, dated to the Early Saxon period. Other investigations have revealed that there were also burials dated to the Romans, Bronze Age and Mesolithic periods; while I had always known that occupation of the downs went way back, I had not expected to find something so precisely where I was looking. This knowledge made me even more determined to go for a walk on the path up the hill, so one fine summer's day in June, Phil and I prepared a picnic lunch, bundled our daughter Holly (who was just a toddler) into the car and drove up to Windmill Down.

We parked the car in the same lay-by the van driver had used back in the winter. I remember staring up the path alongside the field of flowering linseed. Linseed flowers are blue, the wind across a field of linseed in full bloom gives the impression of water, as if you are gazing over a lake – it's a wonderful and atmospheric sight. On Windmill Down, the path was bordered to the left by a fence, with the remains of a thorny hedge straggling upwards. On the right, the blue flowers were brought into sharp focus by the chalky soil beneath. It really was incredibly hot; Holly was happily running ahead of her dad who was lugging the picnic bag up the hill. I was lagging behind, trying to drink in the atmosphere of the place as I puffed and panted in the heat. I reached the halfway point, marked by one of the thorny bushes and stood up straight, easing the kinks out of my back. I remember all of this incredibly clearly, but you're going to have to bear with me on this next bit, because I promise you it happened – and I'm not barking mad!

I stood massaging my back for a moment or two, gazing with fondness at Phil and Holly laughing together further up the path, and then I turned around, facing down the path. The A3 had vanished. The noise of the traffic had been a constant background hum, so constant, so completely normal, that I hadn't noticed it... until now, because it was gone. The only buzz came from the insects and bees, the only other noise came from the wind as it whistled over the turf and scrub. I stood and stared at the rolling landscape; no roads, no Horndean Industrial Estate to the left, no Clanfield to the right. I could see the sparkling waters of the Solent in the distance to my left, but I could not see another human being anywhere. I don't know how long I was stood there, it may have been only a second or two, but it was enough for me to feel more than a bit panicky! I turned to face uphill again and – it all came back; the heat hit me hard and the air felt thicker somehow. The noise of the traffic seemed so loud, but also comforting in a strange way. Best of all though, my husband and daughter were just a few feet away, Phil staring at me in a slightly mystified way. I cannot explain it rationally, but I do believe that for those few seconds, I was in another place – well, the same place, but in a different time. I've been back since, but it only happened the once, and I don't feel the pull to go there in the same way now.

I've tried to analyze the experience, but the only explanation that feels right is that I am somehow connected to these hills and downs, connected perhaps by blood and family going back hundreds or thousands of years. It's another grounding tie, feeling at home in a particular place. I can place myself on that path wherever I am in the world; I can see the view, smell the air, hear the buzz of the A3, or the buzz of the insects in that far off time.

We develop connections to places without even trying; how many of us have said that we feel 'At Home' somewhere that we have visited on holiday. How many of us have fantasized about moving to our favorite holiday locations! We can use this connection in different ways; you've probably heard about putting yourself 'in a different place' when faced with enduring things that may not be that pleasant, but which are necessary, such as going to the dentist. If you can imagine sunning yourself on your favorite beach while sat in the dentist's chair, it has a real proven effect on your ability to feel relaxed, and may even reduce any pain... although with modern anesthetics, it's rare to feel anything! I'm not very comfortable on planes and being able to put myself elsewhere has been absolutely invaluable in helping me overcome my fear.

One method of connecting to that special place is to consciously ground yourself while you are there. Every year when we are in Padstow, I make the effort to build on the connection by meditating and grounding myself there; nobody knows I'm doing it, I'm not wearing a special beach loincloth and I'm not sat cross legged on the sand chanting. I may sit on the sand, or the rocks, I may walk along the beach, or I may stand in the water, it doesn't matter; to anyone passing by, I am just enjoying the scenery. Inside, however, I am visualizing the roots growing from my feet down into the earth, and talking to God about whatever is necessary at that moment. Sometimes, I just stand still and gaze at the scene, committing it to memory. I note the colors, the sounds, the smells, the wind and anything else that will help me remember that place, at that moment. When I need to be there, such as while sitting in a plane waiting for take off, I can put myself there; the power of your mind is such that if you have built the memory in well, you will only have to close your eyes in order for the present moment to fade and for your preferred reality to be almost physical. Reinforcing the connection by visiting somewhere many times and adding layer upon layer of grounding repetition will make the visualization stronger and even more effective. You can also use physical reminders to bring that place into sharp focus. I have a ring with the Vesica Pisces design of interlocking rings found in the Chalice Well Gardens in Glastonbury to remind me of that place, for example. When we travel, I carry a small piece of flint to remind me of my connection to the chalk downs of my home. It's important to keep these in perspective though, or you'll be carrying half the planet around in your bag; I used to carry a rather large obsidian sphere in my handbag when flying – I sometimes wonder what they thought in airport security, but nobody ever challenged me!

I visit Padstow for moments when I need extreme relaxation (is it possible to relax in an extreme manner?) such as when flying or at the dentist. I'm not scared of going to the dentist, but it's nice to be elsewhere when treatment is going on! I visit the Chalice Well Gardens when I need a spiritual boost, or have something important I need to discuss with my Guardian Angels. I have many different places to visit in my mind when I need to – but not all of them are real, physical locations.

The beauty of an internal spiritual life means that you can create anything you like in your mind. If you fancy a marble temple in the stars, filled with angels playing harps, you can; if you prefer a woodland glade, or a tree house, a hobbit burrow or a spaceship, you can. The only limits are in your imagination.

You can build your safe space into which you can retreat in whatever form you want. Take time to think about it, build and rebuild, decorate and redecorate (spiritual Ikea is free!) and make it somewhere truly special. You can go there as often as you like, you can meet your guides, guardians and angels there and it's completely safe.

We all have times when we feel anxious, stressed or depressed; things happen, life happens. As I discuss in the first chapter, facing up to stuff and taking positive action is the best way of fighting it off, but sometimes there seems to be no real reason for how you feel, and that can be a bigger challenge.

Throughout my adult life, I have had periods when I have suffered from anxiety attacks. I know now that I should have gone to the doctor when they first appeared, but over the years I have developed a way of dealing with them that really works for me. On the face of it, there is nothing right now that should cause anxiety attacks; nothing going on that causes me any real worries, but I still find that occasionally one hits me at night, before I go to sleep. The pattern is always the same, I read for a while or play word games with my mum across the net and then, without warning, I become incredibly twitchy. My skin feels as though a million ants are crawling over it, I have a massive hot flush and my heart races. It's horrible; I feel like running around like a headless chicken screaming and tearing my hair, but instead I turn off the light, lie as still as I can and go through my grounding exercises, followed by the chakra routine described in a later chapter. Thankfully, they are few and far between these days.

I was just sixteen the first time I suffered an anxiety attack. It was 1978 and I was Christmas shopping in Westbury Mall, the (then) newly built shopping center in Fareham. I was on my own, happily (!) fighting my way through the crowds of shoppers, when I suddenly began to feel incredibly claustrophobic and panicky. The music was oppressively loud, unrelentingly cheery and the heat overbearing. The crowd seemed to recede into another dimension; I was standing still and alone among a throng of ghostly shapes moving in fast forward. It was very frightening. I remember staggering over to the seating around the fountain; miraculously, there was a space and I collapsed on to it. My breathing was shallow and ragged, I was sweating profusely and I remember my lips feeling cold and tingly despite the heat. I must have passed out because the next thing I recall is waking up; I was lying half on and half off the bench, my head resting on the damp stonework of the fountain, my legs trailing across the floor. My handbag was a few feet away, my shopping scattered around me, kicked about by an uncaring throng of shoppers. Nobody had come to my aid, even though it must have been obvious that I was unwell at the very least! I still find it incredible that not one person felt able to at least see if I needed help; at the very least it's not normal for anyone to let their shopping be kicked about a busy shopping center! This has been, thankfully, the only time I've had such a severe attack, but I still feel anxious occasionally when I'm out and about. I deal with that by consciously breathing slowly, in through the nose, out through the mouth. Not gasping or panting, just slowly breathing normally. At the same time I go through my grounding routine in my mind, and within a few minutes I'm okay.

I appreciate that my attacks are fairly mild; anxiety and panic attacks can be really debilitating; the list of triggers is endless and if you suffer from them, finding out your personal triggers can be the first step to recovery. I don't claim to be a doctor or medical professional; I'm telling you what works for me. I would always advise anyone concerned about their health to consult their doctor.

The deepest levels of grounding can be achieved by under-standing who you are and where you fit into the landscape; there can be many places where you feel that sense of being at home. I love my home city of Portsmouth (somebody has to), Padstow and the rest of Cornwall. There is a mystical atmosphere in many areas of Cornwall which seems to seep out of the landscape. I also love my home and the South Downs, although we had no idea of the depth of family connections when I moved here in the early 1980s.

We ended up living in this area through sheer chance; as I said I had been born in Portsmouth, but grew up near Fareham. It was only when my parents divorced in my teens that my mum and stepdad moved into the Waterlooville and Horndean area – they were in social housing at the time, and had to live where the council sent them. My three children all attended Buriton Primary School, which was nine miles away; my ex lived in the village back then, so it made sense for my eldest son to go there. When I remarried and had two more children, they had to attend the same school because I could not be in two places at once for school runs! It is a lovely school, set against the background of the South Downs, with a large recreation ground complete with cricket pitch behind the school buildings forming a perfect archetypal image of the English Village. It was pure chance that the children ended up here – if my ex had not found accommodation, they would have gone to school elsewhere and it would have been a different story... but it feels as though it was 'meant to be'. I'm wary of using this phrase; I'm also wary of saying 'It's a sign!' as I could see signs in just about anything if I tried hard enough.

A few years ago, we looked at my family history, on my mother's side. My grandmother was still with us then and able to help out where her mother and grandmother were concerned, but beyond that we had to do some digging. Grandma grew up in Titchfield, between Fareham and Southampton, we knew that her mother, Harriet Spencer, had lived in a tiny hamlet called Hogs Lodge, near Clanfield – but you can imagine our surprise when we discovered the strong links with Buriton! Harriet's parents had lived and worked on a farm in the village, many of my ancestors are buried in the churchyard – and it seems that

Harriet may have gone to the village school. Our children had sat in the same classrooms as their great-great-grandmother. To say that I was amazed is an understatement. It seemed that my feelings of being at home in the area were being underlined in history. Of course, this is just one strand of the family; between my mother and father there are connections that stretch the length and breadth of the UK, and right across the world. If you have the opportunity to investigate your own family history, then it can be really worthwhile. Each one of us is a combination of genes, upbringing, experience and that extra indefinable something that makes you unique. Knowing where you have come from is a part of the jigsaw that helps you to understand who you are.

Understanding who you are can take a lifetime, but it's a part of the grounding process.

If you live with your feet on the ground, you have the foundations to reach for the stars.

Chapter 5

Driving on Wheels of Fire

I can remember the first time I read about 'Chakras', an ancient belief that maintains we each have invisible wheels of energy whirling away at different points on our body. I'll be honest: I thought it was a bit farfetched, and although I worked with it, I did not wholeheartedly believe in it!

My opinion changed, however, after I had a profound experience at a charity event to raise funds for the animal charity Blue Cross. A friend had called to ask if I could step in as they had been let down – the snag was it had already started and could I get there really fast! I dashed off in my car and was soon performing tarot and angel card readings in a windy field. Word quickly got around that I was there and I very soon had a long queue stretching across the field. It was so long, that the rest of the event had packed up and gone home by the time I eventually got through it! Towards the end, I began to feel really flaky and a bit spaced out, but I carried on, not wanting to let anyone down.

There were only about half a dozen of people left queuing, and I noticed that they seemed to have colors surrounding them, a bit like the after image you get on the back of your eyelids from gazing at bright lights or strong colors. These colors were not static, however, they were spinning, some faster, some slower, some brighter, some dimmer. A couple of people had darker patches in the colors; something I did not really understand at the time, but which I now interpret as imbalances and issues which need addressing.

The history of belief in a universal energy system is as old as man. It's a proven scientific fact that everything in the universe is made of energy: energy that vibrates in different frequencies and which responds, reacts and interacts. Each of us has our own electromagnetic field, known as the Aura, and each of us has a series of energy centers which relate to our physical, mental, emotional and spiritual well-being.

The Chinese have been writing about this for ten thousand years; they refer to the life force as 'Chi' (pronounced 'Chee') and to the energy centers as 'Meridians'. The Indians, meanwhile, refer to the energy centers as 'Chakras'. Historically, studying the life force was not limited to China and India, although they are the best known traditions; it's something which reaches across the globe.

This life force, Chi, Universal Energy, however you personally refer to it, is at the very heart of many spiritual healing and well-being practices: Reiki, Yoga, Tai Chi, Qigong, Massage, Acupuncture and Acupressure. Martial Arts also focus on the balance and use of the Life Force.

I'm going to focus on the chakra system, as it's the one I'm most familiar with, although I may throw in a bit of Chinese Yin and Yang to boot!

I'll discuss how all this is relevant to your busy life later, but for now, here is the basic structure.

The word 'Chakra' means 'Wheel' in Sanskrit; traditionally there are seven main chakras, although there are many minor ones as well. I'm listing the Sanskrit names as well as the modern Western ones. Acknowledging the chakras and working with them is not difficult – it can be done on the go using the Active Meditation technique described earlier if you wish, but it does have a positive effect on all areas of your life.

1. **Root – Muladhara** is located around the base of the spine. This chakra relates to how grounded you are, how you feel about your Career and Money. A strong Root Chakra means that you are clear about what you want to do and achieve in life, and that you are able to manage money effectively. It also responds to our self-image; when you

look in the mirror, are you happy with what you see? Okay, I know none of us are ever going to be entirely happy... there's always something we'd like to change, but if you review it honestly, how confident are you about how you look? A weak or unbalanced Root Chakra means you may find your work unfulfilling, may feel trapped in the wrong job, may be unsure of what career you really want, or how to achieve it. Money may be an issue too; perhaps you don't have enough for your needs or are trapped into a cycle of overspending and trying to catch up all the time. If you are unhappy with your self-image, this can also be a sign that your Root Chakra needs work.

2. **Sacral – Svadisthana** is located in the lower abdomen below the navel. This chakra deals with our sexuality, which can be a controversial subject! The signs of a strong Sacral Chakra include a healthy attitude to sex and a strong physical relationship with your partner. You are also good at attracting the right people into your life, whether friends or partners, and are seen as someone who can be relied on. However, if you suffer guilt or pain over physical relationships, perhaps have no time or inclination for sex, or find that even when you do make the effort, it feels lackluster, you need to work on this chakra. Other signs of a weak Sacral Chakra include struggling to see yourself as attractive or sexy, feeling worthless, or believing that you will never find the right partner.

3. **Solar Plexus – Manipura** is located at the mid abdomen. The Solar Plexus is your personal power center, channeling energy, drive and determination. If this chakra is strong, you will be a charismatic and confident individual with high levels of self-esteem. You know how to make things happen and you are not afraid to speak

out; you are also generous and able to empower others. A weak Solar Plexus can lead to feelings of hopelessness, questioning yourself and your ability to decide on anything. You may be easily led, and could feel that it 'always happens to you', that you are a victim trapped and unable to make positive changes.

4. **Heart – Anahata** is located in the middle of the chest. The Heart Chakra fuels loving relationships and universal love. Strength shows in self-acceptance, knowing who you are and what is appropriate in comfortable, loving and empathetic relationships with others. You are probably someone that others turn to in times of need, known for your ability to listen and not judge. If you have a weak Heart Chakra, you may sabotage relation-ships because you feel you are not worthy of being loved, or don't deserve it. You may punish yourself for real or imagined wrongdoing, find it difficult to trust others, or commit. You may pick fights or arguments, be unwilling to forgive and be known as a 'prickly' personality, someone who rarely lets their guard down.

5. **Throat – Visuddha** is located at the throat. This is the chakra of your voice, of truth and integrity. A strong Throat Chakra leads to confidence in expressing your opinion, the ability to tackle difficult subjects with discretion and assertion. You will be good at expressing complex thoughts, ideas and plans, admired for your willpower and ability to communicate with everyone at all levels. Your skills enrich your life at every level, from career to home and friends. If your Throat Chakra is weak, you may find it more difficult to express yourself, worried that nobody cares about your opinion anyway. You might be known as the 'Quiet One' and suffer from lack of confidence.

6. **Third Eye – Ajna** is located in the middle of the forehead. The Third Eye or Brow Chakra leads your natural ability to make decisions based on intuition. You may surprise those around you with your ability to pick up on thoughts and feelings, know things without being told, or without knowing quite how you came by that knowledge. You have a clear sense of direction, and those around you are happy to turn to you for advice and guidance. A weak chakra may leave you feeling weak, lost and helpless, uncertain about which direction to take; you may have a history of making disastrous decisions which further undermine your self-confidence as you cannot trust even yourself.

7. **Crown – Sahasrara** is located on the top of the head. The Crown Chakra connects you to God, to the heavens, to spirit and whatever else is up there! A strong chakra means that you feel utterly confident that you are watched over and loved by a higher power and are reminded of it in countless ways on a daily basis. You use positive affirmations to further strengthen your connections and may be described as 'Glowing' by those that know you. The Crown Chakra also connects us to our Higher Selves: that is, the side of us that acts on what is truly good for us, what is true and worthwhile, unblemished by base human instincts! If your Crown Chakra is weak, it can leave you feeling lost and alone, or unworthy of any love from God. You may also feel that you have been abandoned or are being ignored by higher powers, by God, your Guardian Angels, by your loved ones in spirit even.

Each chakra plays a different role in our system and has a specific color or colors associated with it; it takes a little practice to remember it, but is worth the effort. I shall discuss the colors and working with them a bit later. You don't have to sit around in the semi-darkness to work on your chakras either; as I've described in the meditation chapter, you can balance your energy while walking the dog, pushing the buggy or making the bed.

If some of the characteristics of the chakras in a weaker state alarm you, remember that these will all be modified by what's going on with the others. Many years ago, I had real problems with communicating to the partner I was with. We were very short of money, so I would hide things I had bought; if I bought clothes, I would leave them in the boot of the car and sneak them in later when he wasn't around. I'd say my mum had bought them for me! I would also flatly refuse to open any post that looked like a bill. That way I could pretend that everything was fine with our finances. I'm still not brilliant with money, but at least now I admit to myself where my faults are. We can be really adept at convincing ourselves that everything is fine; but deep inside, we do know the truth.

On the surface, this affects the Root and Throat Chakras, but it linked in to the Heart, Solar Plexus and Sacral Chakras too. I felt trapped because I couldn't see a way out of the financial situation, and the worry over money was a major factor in the eventual breakdown of our relationship as neither of us was prepared to face up to it, talk about it or do anything to resolve it.

I've been married to Phil since 1993; we've been through a lot together, and in worse situations than the one I've just described. However, there has been a huge difference in the outcomes because we have faced up to them together, rather than trying to act as though everything is fine. We are still broke though! Think about your life now; what sort of issues are you dealing with, and which chakra might they relate to.

The following is an exercise designed to tap into your higher self to get an aerial view of the current state of your chakras. It's very simple but requires complete honesty from you.

You will need a piece of paper and a pen or pencil. Draw a stick man onto the paper and mark the approximate positions of the chakras with a small dot or circle. This really doesn't require any artistic capability! What you are going to do now is draw or scribble over those dots, and then we shall analyze your drawings. Ideally, you are going to draw quickly and instinctively, which is why there are no colors involved at this stage. The drawings might be small or large, smooth or ragged, untidy scribbles or jagged tangles, circles, squares, triangles, any shape you like! Each chakra drawing may be the same or completely different from the others. Draw what you feel, from deep in your stomach. We are connecting with your higher self, the side of you which speaks your truth and knows what is good for you. I'm going to discuss this higher self and your Inner Voice in more depth in another chapter, but for now just draw. Before you start, focus on each chakra in turn, starting at the bottom, and then draw how you feel your chakras to be right now, at this minute.

It should take no more than a couple of minutes; and when you have finished, go and make yourself a nice cup of tea! Sit down and drink it, preferably with a couple of your favorite biscuits or cookies. This is also a grounding exercise; it's wise to be sure that you are firmly back in the room, and food and drink is a very simple and enjoyable way of achieving this!

There is no right or wrong way to analyze your drawings; once more, you are going to use your inner knowledge, higher self and instinct to be absolutely truthful. It's not as easy as it sounds. As I have said before, we are all masters of deceiving ourselves.

A completely balanced and energized system would have evenly spaced, evenly drawn, evenly sized, nice regular shapes, not too big and not too small. If this is what you have drawn, you are definitely deceiving yourself!

Tiny regular shapes indicate a need to try and control your energy; you may feel unable to relax or speak out, and may suffer from lack of confidence. You may also feel tired and washed out.

Large and overlapping shapes indicate generosity and a big

heart, but also that you may be giving too much of your own energy to others. You also may feel tired, unable to cope with the demands of your life.

Untidy scribbles may be a sign that you feel out of control in one or more areas of your life, or that you have no choice but the course you are on, headed for an inevitable outcome that you may not be comfortable with. It can also denote a need to escape from something or someone holding you back.

Over the years, I have worked through this exercise with many people; here is an example to show how this works in practice. I've changed the name.

This is not a 'reading', like a tarot or angel card psychic reading; it's about guiding and encouraging the individual to recognize where the imbalances lie themselves. If I were to read it for her, it would be my interpretation only; as human beings we tend to rebel against folks telling us what to do. If you genuinely want to change your life, it has to come from you, and unless you recognize your own challenges for yourself, it just won't happen.

Joanne's Chakra drawing showed:

Root Chakra – Big scribbly circle
Sacral Chakra – Tiny scribbly circle
Solar Plexus Chakra – Big scribbly circle
Heart Chakra – Very large, smooth and even heart shape covering most of the page
Throat Chakra – Smooth Spiral of medium size
Brow Chakra – Smooth Spiral slightly smaller than the Throat Chakra
Crown Chakra – Small even circle

I talked to Joanne about her drawing and asked her about each item in turn; the words are mine, but it was Joanne who worked out what the issues were, and faced up to the challenges.

Root Chakra – Joanne was working as a care assistant in a residential nursing home, but wanted to be a nurse. She felt that because she had not done well at school, she wouldn't be taken seriously if she applied. Money was tight at home and she was secretly comfort eating, which had led to her putting weight on, something that was further undermining her confidence. The big scribbly circle showed that she felt out of control and helpless to change the situation.

Sacral Chakra – Joanne was in a loving relationship with two teenage children, but her physical relationship with her partner had dwindled to almost nothing because she felt 'fat and unattractive'. However, she also felt powerless to tackle it. The tiny scribbly circle reflected this.

Solar Plexus – Joanne was constantly tired with trying to run around after her family and had hardly a minute to herself. Her work was physically and emotionally draining, and her energy levels would be very erratic. The big scribbly circle showed how she was using too much of her energy on others and not looking after herself.

Heart Chakra – The huge heart drawing confirmed Joanne's amazing empathy and healing energy, but she wanted to feel more focused and less emotional.

Throat Chakra – Even with so much going on, Joanne is still an excellent communicator. It links in with her Brow Chakra and intuition because of the identical shapes and sizes, showing that she is good at using her intuition, especially when working with those in need of healing. However, she is less effective at communicating her own needs.

Brow Chakra – Joanne has a clear idea of where she wants to be, as shown by the regular drawing; but when combining it with the Root and Solar Plexus, it confirms that she has little confidence about how to go about getting there.

Crown Chakra – The small even circle that Joanne has drawn on her Crown Chakra showed that she wanted very much to be able to believe, but felt that as nothing had shown any interest in her so far, it was probably all rubbish! Joanne also said although she had prayed intermittently throughout her life, she had never felt that anyone was listening.

The above analysis was the result of a couple of weeks of e-mails back and forth and much soul searching for Joanne. Before we talked about ways of strengthening her chakras and working towards resolving her issues, I asked her to perform the exercise again and the results were quite surprising.

The scribbly circles of the lower three chakras had begun to even out, and the sizes were a little more regular, as though just acknowledging things had begun the healing process. The Heart Chakra was still oversized, but slightly smaller, the Throat and Brow Chakras were the same, but the Crown Chakra was now a beautiful half-open flower. Joanne said that she had consciously decided that she would believe in a higher power and was asking for help, although she was keeping an open mind for the time being!

Joanne decided that the main issues were:

Wanting to follow her heart and become a qualified nurse. Reconnecting physically with her partner. Learning to love herself – no matter how she looked, but also losing weight. Finding more time for herself. Finding her soul.

Her confidence was growing all the time as she researched what she would need to do to become a nurse, and this in turn helped her be more assertive at work, able to say no when she was too tired to carry on and do more hours. She also carried this forward into her personal life, organizing the children to take on some of the chores and encouraging her partner to do some of the running around in the evenings taking the kids from place to place. Joanne also talked honestly to her partner about how she had been feeling and asked for his support, something which was gladly given. A year after our initial discussions, Joanne contacted me again to tell me that she had lost three stones in weight and had just applied to be a nurse. She felt great and was on top of the world; she had also worked on talking to her Guardian Angel and had received what she saw as a fantastic sign that she was on the right path!

Of course this has been simplified ('sequences have been shortened' as they say on the mobile phone advertisements on the telly!), but it's a great example of how an honest appraisal of where you are right now together with positive action can improve your life. It doesn't require any meditation techniques at all if you prefer not to; just an open mind and a wholehearted approach.

I mentioned earlier about the color associations; you'll discover that there are different ideas about what color goes with which chakra; for the most part, I use the most commonly known ones, but you may find that it works better for you with slightly different shades. It's a personal thing.

Root Chakra	Red
Sacral Chakra	Orange
Solar Plexus Chakra	Yellow
Heart Chakra	Pink and Green
Throat Chakra	Blue
Brow Chakra	Violet
Crown Chakra	Sparkling Shimmering Crystal

I use this quick fix chakra meditation to help me stay on an even keel from day to day, or hour to hour, or minute to minute... I usually do it while walking, or last thing at night before going to sleep.

First, imagine roots growing from the soles of your feet, which burrow their way right to the magma at the center of the earth in a flash. Next, imagine some of that hot magma energy flowing back up through the roots to the soles of your feet. It may feel warm, but not uncomfortably so. At this point, you have to be able to remember the sequence and colors of the chakras which, as I've said, can take a little practice.

The energy flows up your legs and into the Root Chakra. Imagine each chakra as a ball which opens like a flower bud and then spins or whirls; for the Root, the flower is red and whirls relatively slowly. The energy then climbs up to the Sacral Chakra, opening a vibrant orange flower, which spins a little faster than the red one. Next it moves on to the Solar Plexus Chakra, opening a vivid golden yellow flower and spinning a little faster again. On to the Heart Chakra and a flower of alternating pink and green, spinning a little faster than the Solar Plexus. The energy rises again, to the Throat Chakra, where a flower of turquoise and cobalt blues blooms and whirls, again a little faster than the previous Heart Chakra. Up once more to the Brow Chakra and a flower of mystical violet, spinning a little faster than the Throat Chakra. Finally, the energy activates the crystal white shimmering lotus bloom of the Crown Chakra, which spins faster than any of the other chakras. It then continues upwards, connecting you from the center of the Earth, to the heavens above. In the chapter on angels I'll show you how you can intensify this connection.

It's a simple method of activating, acknowledging and balancing the chakra energies for everyday purposes, taking very little time. It can have the effect of helping you to feel calmer, more connected and better able to cope with the demands of the day.

You can also affect individual chakras as you wish; for

example, if you are going for an interview, you might want to boost your communication skills and Throat Chakra. One way of doing this is to wear something blue, or carry something blue with you. I use crystals for this; there are some suggestions below on which crystals to use, but this is not an exhaustive list. To boost an individual chakra, I will complete the above exercise and then focus my attention on the specific chakra I need, while holding a piece of Turquoise, or Blue Sodalite for example. You don't need complicated language or rituals, just hold the thought and the focus of what you want to achieve.

Root Chakra – Red – Smokey Quartz, Garnet, Mahogany, Obsidian

Sacral Chakra – Orange – Carnelian, Moonstone, Aragonite

Solar Plexus Chakra – Yellow – Citrine, Orange Calcite, Yellow Jasper

Heart Chakra – Pink/Green – Rose Quartz, Green Aventurine, Malachite

Throat Chakra – Blue – Turquoise, Sodalite, Blue Calcite

Brow Chakra – Violet – Amethyst, Iolite, Azurite

Crown Chakra – Clear/White – Clear Quartz, Selenite, Clear Calcite

Of course, if you feel like splashing out on gemstones, then Tourmaline, Ruby, Topaz, Emerald, Sapphire, Amethyst and Diamond might have to do... but thankfully, you don't have to spend a fortune as tumble stones, and uncut rough stones will work just as well! Mankind has been collecting shiny stones since the dawn of time; some of the most ancient grave goods are beads made from Amber and Turquoise. Today, crystals are readily available from New Age and mineral shops, both on the high street and online. If possible, try to buy your crystals from a high street shop so that you get the chance to handle them first; it's strange but true that some stones seem to call out to you...

I have been working with crystals for many years now; I have a dedicated set of stones for chakra use just for me. I've discovered that it helps me if I know what I'm working with to the extent that I no longer need the actual crystals with me in order to work with them. I know what they look like, the colors, the shapes and the feel of them. So if I'm out and about and need an energy boost, I can imagine I'm holding the Citrine against my Solar Plexus, or visualize my gorgeous Orange Calcite angel statue that lives on my desk. When I was working on other people, I had many different stones and would select them based on what felt right.

Now you cannot go around blaming everything on your chakras; I can just imagine the reaction if I called in sick because I needed to balance and energize my chakras! However, learning to recognize the signs when something is out of balance or needs attention is a useful skill.

Recognizing that something is wrong might be easy, after all, anyone can tell when I'm in a bad mood for example; but what about putting it right? The simplest methods can be the best, and if you are hurtling through your day, the chances are you won't have time to book an appointment with your local therapist, so here is my solution.

1. Identify where you think the issue is rooted. You will know, after all, this is your body, your energy system, and if you cannot remember the names or locations of those pesky chakras it doesn't matter. Think about how you feel, and where you think that feeling is rooted.
2. Imagine a bright beam of sunshine illuminating your whole body. In your mind, you are going to see it gently warming you, so that any areas of your energy that feel or look cloudy will be regenerated and reenergized.
3. If you are aware of specific chakra issues, relating to the properties listed above, then you can visualize each

chakra in turn, becoming larger or smaller, faster or slower, as you feel it needs to be. This is the most important thing: Your energy, Your body, Your decisions.

If you do visit a therapist, then they will talk to you and professionally assess your issues based on the information you share, and what they pick up on through their senses, tuned into your energy, but YOU know your body best. Learning to work with, balance and energize your own chakra system can be very effective.

Chapter 6

The Cosmic Superstore

I firmly believe that if we want something to happen, we have to help it along. It's no good hoping that everything is going to fall into our laps without any positive action from us. It's a bit like hoping to win the lottery but never buying a ticket. At the same time I know from personal experience that if we want something passionately enough, the universe can sometimes step in. I'll come back to that.

Following an accident in 1995, I began to develop my creative skills, painting brightly colored designs onto ceramics. I thought I could develop a business from it and asked the universe for help finding customers. I also began actively looking for places that might be suitable for selling my work. Almost immediately opportunities came my way, but they did not manifest out of thin air, I still had to do some work myself. I believe that the universe helps those who help themselves, so perhaps it worked because the right people looked at my designs, or were in the right frame of mind when I approached them. I was never approached by someone saying, "We simply must sell your stuff!"

Actually, that's not quite true. I took a phone call about two years after I started selling the ceramics from a USA cable shopping channel who wanted my products. I had been placing my order in the Cosmic Superstore for more orders, so initially I was thinking Yippee! You've cracked it girl! There was, however, a tiny snag. My Inner Voice was laughing maniacally as I tried to explain that there was no way I could supply them with 12,000 of each product, all hand painted by me and fired in our family gas cooker!

I began by selling at local craft fairs and shops and then ventured further afield, doing events in London and supplying a shop in Glastonbury. We also adapted my website to sell my work, and I undertook commissions for special pieces. I started off painting simple fruit designs but quickly moved on to different subjects: Hares, Dragons, Unicorns – and the Green Man. My best known illustrations are the Green Man images on dishes, bowls, mugs and plates – if you have something with Pennymoon written somewhere on the bottom, it's one of mine! I'm really proud of what I achieved in that time and you can see photos of my work on my website. However, it became apparent that I would never be able to paint enough to make a living; each item had about 8–10 layers of paint and although I painted them in bulk, when I broke it down it worked out at around a ½ hour to complete one mug, much longer for the bigger pieces. I was never going to be able to sell them for enough to make it worthwhile for anything but a hobby. If you are one of the many craftspeople around the country who sell your goods, you will know what I mean. The mug cost at least 75p (50 cents) back then, and the most we could sell them for was £7.50 ($5). If I sold them to shops, I only made around half the selling cost. I had to include the costs of paint, brushes, fuel, stall costs and all the rest of it, and it was just not viable. I began to diversify into crystals and put together my own Crystal Healing Kits. I also began performing tarot and angel readings at events, but was still only just about breaking even. It was great fun, but tough at the same time.

When I took part in Mind, Body and Spirit events I liked wandering around to talk to other stallholders. I was amazed that some of them did no form of marketing or advertising at all, and some seemed to struggle with talking to customers too. It reminded me of the first craft fair I ever did, back in 1989. My eldest son was not even a year old at the time and I was still on maternity leave from my job. I have always loved making my own jewelry and thought I might be able to make some extra cash from it. I spent ages making earrings, bracelets and necklaces, and went off to the event happy in the knowledge that when all of it sold I would be £300 better off. I had not considered how to display it on the table, or that my taste might not be the same as other people's! I came home feeling really dispirited, having sold a fraction of what I had made. It was an important lesson and I vowed that next time I would be better prepared. I never went back to sell jewelry and I still have many of the items now, stored in my jewelry-making cabinet, waiting to be broken up and reused.

I decided to try to help the stallholders who were finding the marketing aspects difficult, and I put together a workshop. It was a real eye-opener – many traders felt that they did not need to advertise in any way and did not need an online presence because they believed that the universe would bring people (customers) to them. Now while the organizers of the events would advertise, I argued that surely they wanted or needed customers between the events! Some people felt that a website wasn't for them because they were worried about chat rooms! I was amazed that anyone in business could not agree that giving their customers the ability to see their goods and get in touch 24/7 via e-mail was a good idea. Even when they admitted that the Internet was their own first choice when looking for goods or services, some still could not see how it applied to their own business. The fear of somehow being stalked via the Internet from folks who were giving out business cards with their name and address on was mind-boggling. This taught me another important lesson. You can only sell what people want. Find out what your customers want before you even think of starting out. I wanted to show the stallholders effective practical methods of bringing in customers, but what most of them wanted were customers that required little or no effort on their part.

Of course, times have now changed, and I would hope that anyone going into business today would agree that an online presence, no matter how basic, is essential. An open mind is also essential; whatever your work, whatever is happening in your life, a mind open to new ideas and evolution will always take you forward.

Meanwhile, back in the Cosmic Superstore, how can you place your order and be sure of getting what you want? Cosmic Ordering, or the principle of 'Ask and you shall receive' has been with us for a very long time, as long as we have been praying to a higher power.

I'm a regular shopper in the superstore, although sometimes I don't realize I'm in there! Remember my impassioned plea for a tummy tuck? I got it... but in a way I could never have imagined. I do not subscribe to the belief that I somehow brought breast cancer upon myself, although there are books out there that will tell you that subconsciously I did, through my actions, inactions, and energy imbalances. I'm only human and I'll be honest with you, I found it difficult to deal with enough, without having folks tell me that it was somehow my fault!

One thing I do accept was that it was a message that I needed to slow down again, take stock and change my direction of travel. I knew that I wanted to work for myself, and that I wanted to be involved in Mind, Body and Spirit, (or 'Weirdy Stuff', as the kids called it) and as the holistic events with crystals and readings didn't seem to be paying enough, I decided to undertake training in healing therapies. A quick search online for Reiki training kept on bringing up the same site, based in Glastonbury, and I took this as a sign that I was on the right track!

It's not a good idea to rely entirely on those pesky 'signs'; proper groundwork always pays off, but I had a wonderful time qualifying as a Reiki Master. It was just unfortunate that my qualification was not recognized by any industry governing bodies, which meant that I could not get insurance to practice on the public! I decided to train as a fully qualified Spiritual Healer with a recognized organization, and also to undertake training in Indian Head Massage and Hopi Ear Candling. I passed the last two with flying colors and was nearing the end of my healer training when my cancer diagnosis was made. This was a bitter blow at the time, as I had been about to start practicing on people in the foundation clinics; now I had to put everything on hold while I recovered and healed myself.

Whatever that higher power is, it knows what it's doing. If I had qualified, would I be writing this now? Probably not. Would it be the right path for me? Probably not, in retrospect. I have friends who have gone on to become very successful healers and I know that it's not an easy ride, with the ever present risk of personal burnout. There were personal benefits to the training, so it was the right thing for me to do when I did it, but it was not right for me to continue doing it. I could argue that the healer training prepared me in many ways to endure the cancer treatments; I believe that using self-healing techniques in the days and weeks after chemotherapy or surgery helped me to recover both physically and spiritually. Chemotherapy in particular (or the art of almost completely poisoning the patient in order to heal them) had what I felt at the time was a dreadful effect on my spiritual well-being. I felt disconnected and cut off; my Reiki healing routines helped me feel that I had an open link with spirit, even if it was almost undetectable.

One of the most amazing properties of the Cosmic Superstore is that you only ever fill your trolley with the things you need. You cannot overspend or buy shoes that don't fit, because when you get to the checkout those things you don't need have simply vanished! Of course, you might not realize that you don't have them with you, because you're down here still wishing for them, but trust me, if it's not right for you, you don't get it.

I'll discuss in Chapter 9 what happened in 1995, when we had a major motorcycle accident and my career was ended abruptly. I also talked about how my husband was made redundant when the company he was working for went under, but I didn't explain how we got out of the mess we were in financially. After three months of living without an income, Phil went back to work for the same company, but we felt that the writing was on the wall for them and were really worried about the future. We talked about it at length – you know how it goes – you discuss something, analyze it, pick it apart, and do absolutely nothing to resolve it, but also during that time we kept on wishing out loud for a bolt from the blue to save us!

The bolt came when Phil took a call from a friend he had worked with some years previously when he was a commissioning engineer. It seemed that this chap was now quite senior in the company – and wanted to talk to Phil about the possibility of his coming back to work for them. We could not believe it; our prayers had been answered! They came to us for the interview; our youngest child was only a few months old then, so they dutifully stared at the bundle in the pram and then went off to the pub for the 'interview'. He started back with them soon afterwards. Of course everything comes with a price, and the price of commissioning is that the work is based anywhere that needs your services. Phil was working all over the country and sometimes abroad, while I was at home with three young children. That was tough, I felt like a single parent at times, but we talked to each other at least once every day and treasured our time spent together. I'm lucky that I have good friends and my mum and grandma were always there when I needed them. Any stay at home mum will tell you that you need to talk to grownups sometimes; I would have gone stark staring mad if my only conversation had been with young children! I had times when I was so tired I hardly knew what I was doing – and I wasn't even going out to work then!

One of my more bizarre moments occurred on a school run to Buriton. I was late (of course) and the children had already gone in when I arrived. I parked on the end of the yellow zigzags (I know this is not allowed!) as close as possible to the school gates, flung the door open, dragged the boys from the car and shooed them into the school. I then calmly got into the back of the car, and sat there, waiting for someone to drive me home! I must have sat there for about five minutes before I remembered I was the driver!

After a few years commissioning, Phil accepted an offer from a company to stay on as an engineer, looking after the equipment he had just helped install. He stayed there for more than ten years, although it meant commuting into the center of London for work. In late 2010, he was made redundant again and had to face the prospect of finding work in a very different world to the one he had last faced as an unemployed person. By then he was almost 50 too (as was I, we were both born in late 1961) and was worried about being discriminated against on the basis of his age. I know it's not supposed to happen, but we all know that it still does. My first suggestion was to call the commissioning company, but initially he wasn't sure; understandably, he felt embarrassed and a bit sheepish about asking to come back.

I suggested that he should put in his order with the Cosmic Superstore, but Phil's not quite as unhinged as I am, so if he did, he was a bit more circumspect than I was! I was asking for help every day; after my previous experiences with uncontrolled wishes, I was very careful about how I asked for help too. In 1995, I just wanted out of my situation. I felt guilty about letting everyone down and could not see a way through at all, so I just wished to be free of it. My wish was granted with a major accident that gave me time with the kids (very positive), but ended my career (negative). It opened up my creative talents and helped me reconnect to the universe (positive), but caused me lots of pain which is still ongoing 18 years later (Negative? Maybe, maybe not.).

When I wished passionately for a tummy tuck with no idea of how to achieve it, my wish was granted when I was diagnosed with breast cancer. I had the tummy tuck (positive), but had to endure chemotherapy (negative). It ended my healing career before it even began (negative), but started my career in writing (positive).

All of the 'negatives', by the way, are only negative if taken out of context, or not in conjunction with the many blessings which outweigh them. I view everything that has happened in my life as a blessing – even if it was not immediately obvious what that blessing was.

When Phil was made redundant I began the list for the Cosmic Superstore.

'Please can you arrange for Phil to get another job as soon as possible, preferably one that is close by, and means he will be home every night. It has to pay enough for the bills too. I don't want anyone to suffer anything bad as a result of him getting the job either. Thank you.'

Phil had registered with various engineering recruitment agencies and a few months' work with a view to permanent came in quite quickly. It was less than 20 miles from home too, so I had high hopes. I say "I had high hopes" because it was apparent from the start that Phil hated it. He was so far out of his comfort zone that he could have been working on the moon. It wasn't in his field of expertise either, but he did his best. He was fairly sure that he would not be asked to stay on and this is what happened. I did my best to pick him up, but he was feeling really down after he left.

I gently suggested (well, nagged, if I'm honest) for him to call the commissioning company again and, eventually, he did. We were both disappointed when he was told that they'd love to consider having him back – if they had a suitable vacancy, but that in the years since he had left, the landscape had changed out of all recognition and, of course, times were tough there too. It was more difficult to help pick him up from this news, but I did my best. He applied for loads of jobs, but no interviews were forthcoming. Phil even applied for a job with a fish processing plant, despite having a violent distaste of fish and anything that smells even remotely of fish! He goes green if I as much as grill a fish finger, so how he imagined he was going to be able to work in a fish processing plant with all the attendant fishy pongs is anybody's guess!

Meanwhile, I was putting in my order again.

'Okay, so I appreciate the last one didn't work out, but thank you so much for putting it his way. Can you somehow arrange for him to go back to the other company please? I don't want anyone to be harmed in the fulfilling of this wish, but it seems to be the best option for us. If it's not possible, please can you help with something else that pays enough for us to be able to pay the bills with a bit left over, and that he likes doing? We need it to happen before everything goes completely tits up here as well. Thank you for any help, it's appreciated.'

I was doing this every day, every morning as I got up and every night as I went to bed, trying to be positive all the time, but it was beginning to look ever more grim financially. He had been made redundant in November, and had only had that few months' work since, which had ended in May. By August, we were really worried, but there was a glimmer of hope in two interviews he attended. We were in the supermarket when he took a call that made him go deathly white. It sounded positive, but I wasn't sure... it felt like a very long time before he eventually ended the call. It wasn't related to either of the two companies who were interviewing him; it was the commissioning company, wondering if he was still looking for a job? For the second time, they saved us from sleeping in a tent! It seemed someone had left, more work had come in and they needed Phil back. Hallelujah! I had visions of angels manifesting job opportunities for this other chap so that he was happy before he could move on to getting Phil back where he wanted to be! Patience may be a virtue, but it was really close. We reckon we had about a month left in the kitty before we would have had to put the house on the market.

He's happy, so I'm happy. He has to work away most of the time of course, but also seems to spend a fair bit of time at home, which is wonderful.

I am working at three different jobs right now, and happy to do so. I work for Waterstones, the national chain of bookshops, with a wonderful group of people and love every moment of it. I also run a large Slimming World group in Portsmouth; I never thought I'd ever join a weight loss class, let alone find myself working for them less than six months later! I've been helping people achieve their target weights for more than five years now and it's an incredibly rewarding experience. I'm also lucky enough to be writing successfully. I've worked very hard at it, but I've also had my fair share of challenges. At one point, I never thought this book would ever be finished; my initial estimate of three months to write it has stretched into almost two years, and I've ignored all the little digs from my Inner Voice until now to get my act together. Life likes to throw the odd spanner in the works and several things have happened to throw me temporarily off course recently, which I talk about in Chapter 8, The What If Factor. It took another delivery from the Cosmic Ordering Superstore to get me back on track. I placed my order for a week's peace and quiet to get things finished off, but I forgot to ask for that week to be completely clear of any dramas or issues in the family! I had decided to spend Sunday clearing my mind, and clearing the decks at home; all the washing was done, nothing needed cleaning desperately, and I had already sorted out the garden for the summer. I went to bed Sunday night with the warm fuzzy feeling of someone who was going to be able to spend the whole week doing what she had planned.

At 2.00am, my phone rang. Son No. 2 was ill and needed help. He was only in the adjoining bedroom (some years ago, we bought three brass handbells at a school fete, so that when the children were ill, they could ring them if they needed us. Now they just text!), but was throwing up and felt worried. Phil, bless him, went to sort him out, knowing that I was desperate to get some proper rest so that nothing would stand in the way of my writing. By the morning, however, even I was worried (I'm not going to go into the gory details!) and called the doctor. The doctor reassured me, and I did get some work done, but not as much as I would have liked. I amended my order and requested that nobody became ill, or suffered in any way. The writing progressed well, with a break to run my Slimming World group on Wednesday evening. Thursday evening, another unforeseen spanner (wrench) clanged into the machinery. Despite my foolish belief that I had finished with homework when I left school in 1978, I have done more homework since then than I ever did while at school. On that Thursday, it seemed that I was required to assist with our daughter's GCSE Drama work. The exam board had added an extra couple of elements to her already crowded revision schedule and she was beyond tired already. She had been doing her GCSEs with a rotten cold and could hardly speak, something which doesn't help in French verbal exams, or indeed, when you are required to sing for the Drama GCSE! It took us about five or six hours of hard work to research the added work and I now know more about the 'Naturalism' theatre movement than I ever feel I needed to. In case you're interested, it came to prominence in the 1870s and focuses on portraying the very lowest orders of civilization struggling with a terribly poor existence and completely failing to rise above it. Lovely. I amended my order again. It's a bit like placing an online grocery shopping order and finding they are out of bananas but send you broccoli instead. I ordered peace and quiet surely, what's all this other stuff? Dealing with the daily distractions of life and still achieving what you want is a real talent and I'll tell you how I manage that, too, in Chapter 8, The What If Factor. I don't always succeed of course, as I say throughout this book, anyone who claims to have a perfect life is not being honest with themselves. If you can identify the things that are urgent and need your attention NOW, and accept that some things may need to be done later, you are winning, and although I could have told

Holly to go off and get on with it herself, of course I was not going to do it. This was a time-sensitive situation, something that could not be put off until tomorrow and it would have been heartless and cruel to turn her away. Our happiness can sometimes rely on the happiness of others in a positive way; I went to bed that night outwardly grumbling about how long it had taken (and how depressing the subject matter was) but inwardly I had the warm fuzzy glow of knowing that I had done everything in my power to help.

The list of situations that we call for help with is infinitely long, but the subjects broadly fall into just a few categories.

1. 'Please help me, I'm broke!' I'm putting money at the top because it can cause such pain, from mild anxiety to sheer terror. I had a situation some time ago in which my blood actually ran cold. We've all heard the expression 'it made my blood run cold' but I did not think it was something that could happen physically until it happened to me. I had recently opened a new bank account for my business and the first payment to come out of the account had bounced; I opened the post that morning with a happy heart and as I read the letter from the bank, the most horrible feeling shot around my body. It felt like ice in my veins and left me breathless, clammy and scared. Where on earth had my money gone? It hadn't gone anywhere of course. The bank had made a mistake! It took them a while to admit it of course, but four months later I finally got a letter of apology. My situation was trivial compared to others' but it still frightened the life out of me. We all deserve a life with enough money to be comfortable. Twenty years ago I was wishing to be wildly wealthy; today I am wishing for enough for my needs. I would like enough money to pay the bills, live in my home, look after

my loved ones and have a bit left over for a rainy day. A lottery win would be nice of course, but I'm not wishing for that; I am happy to work hard to achieve my dreams. Regardless of what has gone before, and how much you want, before you wish for money, know precisely what your position is now. Face up to things. Work out the practical steps you can take now to improve things or find the extra money you need, and ask for professional help if you need it.

2. 'Please help me to find love!' If you want a new partner, you are going to have to go out there and meet people. According to many surveys, the top methods of meeting that special person are through friends, social activities with friends and family, and work, school or college. Online dating comes a poor last. That special person could be staring at the stars right now and wishing to meet you; it would be a shame if your paths never crossed because you had to stay in and wash your hair! I met Phil through a friend; I was recently divorced and out of touch with life, so I got a bar job at a local pub. I was invited round to his house for after hours drinks one evening with a crowd and had bought some beer to share; as I went down the steps to the front door, I missed the threshold and stumbled, falling into Phil's arms. My wonderful husband's first ever words to me were "Watch out! You'll ruin that beer!"… and they say romance is dead!

3. 'Please help my loved ones!' It's completely right and natural to want the very best for those we love and every prayer, every wish, is heard.

4. 'Please help me find my dream job.'

Here are some things to consider then before placing your order in the Cosmic Superstore.

1. Be as specific as you can (or want), about exactly what you want. Releasing a vague or woolly wish into the ether is either not going to work, or may work in a way you had never imagined – and may not want.

2. Face up to what is happening in your life right now. Wishing for a happy ending won't work unless you begin to take positive action to get the ball rolling.

3. Remember to stay positive and accept with joy all the blessings already in your life.

4. Be patient. Other things may have to happen in order for you to get what you want. We had to wait for the other guy to leave, before Phil could go back to his old company.

5. Don't be scared to ask for signs. I know I have said that I am careful where signs are concerned, but sometimes they are unmissable – as long as you are looking for them! Read the chapter on angels to see what I mean.

6. It is really necessary? Do you really need to ask the universe to make sure it doesn't rain on your washing? Save your requests for the things that are really important to you.

7. Be prepared to work for it too. Don't think that the universe will shower you with gifts without you ever lifting a finger. While waiting for your request to be granted, continue to look proactively for ways of helping yourself, for example by trying to meet new people if you are looking for a new partner. Be confident! Shine like the star you are and people will be drawn to you like a magnet. Make an effort.

8. If you have a specific timescale during which things need to happen, don't be afraid of putting that bit in.

9. Ask for help from friends, relatives, colleagues and the authorities if you need it. While the universe works behind the scenes, don't let things drag on.

10. Do not, ever, wish harm on another person, or wish for your situation to be resolved at the expense of others.
11. It's no good wishing to win the lottery. It doesn't work like that.
12. Be passionate! Wishy-washy wishes won't wash.
13. It's always polite to say please and thank you.
14. Last but not least, be careful of what you might unleash on an unsuspecting world!

I'm putting that last bit in because of the fairies we have at home. I cannot explain this next bit, and it's still going on, but I promise you I'm not nuts. Probably.

My best friend is a wonderful lady called Tracey. We have known each other for more than 30 years and have always dreamt of co-owning a business. We haven't quite achieved this yet although we haven't given up! One of our ideas was an aromatherapy business called 'Away with the Faeries'. We bought several gallons of Sweet Almond base oil, and lots of different concentrated oils to blend with it. We then researched in depth the properties of dozens of oils so that we could produce our own, unique, blends.

The only thing was, we needed to be able to justify our claim that these were Faery Oils; what could we do…?

We decided that we should go up in the forests of the Queen Elizabeth Country Park and connect with the local Faeries, and ask them to bless our Faery Oils! It sounded like a completely rational idea to us, and we told our long-suffering husbands that they would be required to haul the gallons of sweet almond oil up the steep slopes into the forest, where we would then connect with the local faeries and very carefully and respectfully ask them to bless the oils, and our venture. To their credit, Phil and Ross didn't even bat an eyelid… they knew us too well to be anything other than resigned, but they definitely cheered up when we told them we would take them to the pub afterwards to connect with the local beer!

Tracey and I had found a poem in an old book that claimed to be able to call or invoke faeries which seemed to suit our purpose, although it was not without some challenges. The first was the need for a green cord, exactly nine feet in length, which had to be tied around a central tree, or post, and then around your foot. We weren't sure if that meant nine feet clear between the post and the foot, or nine feet overall, and then tie it on the post and foot; we decided to go for nine feet overall. We also needed some music on a flute or pipe; Ross has a penny whistle, so he was press-ganged into playing that, while Phil was instructed in the art of walking around in a circle with a nine-foot length of green cord tied around one foot. We also thought we ought to take some offerings for the faeries, so we took a picnic, for us and for them. Do faeries like pork pies and scotch eggs? We're still unsure on this tricky question.

That beautiful summer evening was one of the most entertaining of my life; we drove up to the edge of the forest on the downs and parked. Phil and Ross carried the several gallons of oil, Tracey and I carried the food and other paraphernalia up the steep slopes deep into the forest. Now the thing with the Queen Elizabeth Country Park is that it's a very popular place to walk, especially on a fine summer evening, and we wanted to be sure of complete privacy. If you are going to attempt to invoke faeries, it's probably better done in private, so we walked and walked until we were sure that no other walkers would be able to find us. Eventually, we discovered a beautiful glade, with a centrally placed young tree ideal for tying a nine-foot length of cord to. There was even a fallen tree we could use as a bench. Tracey and I placed the oils near our bench and tied one end of the cord to the tree, and the other end to Phil. He wasn't keen on having it tied to his foot as he felt he would trip up, so it ended up tied around his waist, which made the cord substantially shorter than nine feet but what the hey. Ross produced his penny whistle, and

Tracey and I began declaiming in ringing tones our poem "Strange Music echoes through the glade..." That was as far as we got; the music coming from Ross was indeed strange, and we got the giggles. It's really tricky trying to declaim anything in ringing tones when there are tears of laughter running down your cheeks! It wasn't helped by Phil, who had really got into the spirit of things by doing an impression of Quasimodo, lurching in a drunken manner around the tree dragging one foot behind him and muttering "The Bells, the bells..." under his breath. The cord wasn't slipping around the tree either; it was caught firmly on something, which meant that Phil was moving in smaller and smaller circles as the cord wrapped around the trunk, until eventually he collapsed against it! By now, Ross had given up any attempt at his strange music and the only sound echoing around the glade was helpless laughter; we were just managing to regain control when a car appeared! It was about 50 yards away and higher up the down – in our efforts to walk as far as possible into the forest to escape the walkers, we had managed to park ourselves next to the only road winding across the back of the down, in a spot guaranteed to give drivers and passengers the optimum view of our antics. Needless to say, that set us off again...

The business never really got off the ground; the Internet was still in its infancy, and social networking, eBay and PayPal still unknown, and after a few months, we moved on to different things, but one thing we definitely achieved, and that was invoking the faeries.

Since that evening, we have had a series of completely unexplainable events here at home, and even occasionally on holiday. We have accepted that we have 'Faeries' living with us, although you may think differently. The first incident occurred not long after that evening. We went to visit my mum and, on our return, casually dropped a carrier bag containing half a packet of biscuits, lots of crumbs and a couple of the kids' toys in the doorway to the dining room. When it vanished the following day, we didn't really think anything of it, just assumed that someone had moved it – although we looked everywhere to find it without success. About three weeks after it disappeared, it came back, in the very spot it had been left, still containing the half-packet of biscuits, the crumbs and the toys. If one of the kids had moved it, the biscuits would have gone, trust me! It was odd, but we forgot it – until a couple of months later when Phil was putting filing into plastic sleeves. He was sat at the back of the living room, and I was sorting some stuff out in the conservatory, which involved my walking back and forth past where he was working. There was a huge and untidy pile of plastic sleeves on the floor; they were really slippery, and I was concerned that I was going to do myself a mischief, so I shouted to him to please move them. Less than five minutes later, he asked me where I had put his plastic sleeves. I had not touched them, but they were gone, vanished into the ether and never to return. We cannot even begin to explain this, and if anyone has any sensible ideas not involving faeries, I'd be pleased to consider them. Then there was the incident with the suitcase belonging to my mum-in-law. May moved down from Liverpool to live with us some years ago; she regularly visits friends and family back home and has a distinctive blue suitcase with some green raffia tied onto the handle to help identify it in airports.

She came back from Liverpool with the suitcase, but the next time she needed it, it was nowhere to be found. We looked in all the places that would fit a large case, and lots that would not, but to no avail. The faeries had made off with it and, eventually, she bought another one. Some months later, my eldest son James asked why we had put a large blue case in his wardrobe… Even more bizarre was the fact that he had performed one of his regular clear-outs in his room and wardrobe within the last couple of weeks and it had not been in there then!

These are just a small selection of our Faery-related incidents.

I appreciate that you are probably reading this and saying that there has to be a rational explanation, but honest, we've tried and failed to come up with one. I truly believe that, somehow, our mucking about in the forest caused us to bring something back home; I'm very careful to treat them nicely and be respectful, or who knows what might happen!

Shopping in the Cosmic Superstore is best done when you are sober and in full possession of your senses. Be specific and, above all, make sure you ask that only good should come to everyone as a result of your 'shopping'. Don't forget, that you do have to make an effort yourself; there's an old proverb that goes, 'God Helps Those Who Help Themselves'. Which means that if you are taking positive action, you will get there much quicker, if at all.

I would not be writing this now if I had not stepped right out of my personal comfort zone. In the wake of the breast cancer, I had a serious think about where I saw myself in years to come. Writing was something I have always loved, and after the years spent painting thousands of images of the Green Man, there was a definite advantage in that it only had to be done once, before you moved on to the next article, or book. The challenge lay in knowing how to get started. There was a moment when I decided to try; it was at the beginning of the kids' half-term holiday in October 2005. We were staying in Cornwall because I had this strong feeling that I absolutely had to be working at this particular MBS event in Penzance – and Phil is such a daft and wonderful person, that he arranged for us to spend the week in Padstow, even though we couldn't really afford it.

Sadly for the organizers, the MBS event clashed with a major festival of the sea in the town, with the result that numbers attending were low. I was performing tarot and angel readings; and just opposite me, was a stand selling all manner of angel paraphernalia, belonging to Jacky Newcomb. I knew of Jacky, she had written several books on angels and was known as

'Jacky the Angel Lady'; I was trying to pluck up the courage to talk to her. She seemed really friendly, chatting to customers and stallholders alike, but I was unaccountably nervous and just couldn't do it. The first day ended and we all went back to our lodgings; I told Phil that Jacky was there and he just said, "Go and talk to her; what's the worst that can happen?" He was right of course, but it took me until 3.00pm on that second and final day before I went over. I don't remember what I said to start with, but somehow I managed to ask how she got started in writing; her advice was straightforward and sound, and she was really friendly. Jacky and her husband John are firm friends now and I shall be forever grateful to her for her support. Jacky suggested writing articles for magazines as a way of getting started; she pulled no punches and said I should be prepared for lots of rejection letters, but the very next weekend I had another stroke of luck. I was working at another event, this one in Haslemere, Hampshire; there was a chap there promoting his daughter's book… and as I chatted to him about my own writing ambitions, it turned out that he knew of a new magazine looking for writers! It seemed that my orders were being fulfilled faster than I had anticipated. I wrote a sample article, e-mailed it to the editor, and she took it! I was amazed to say the least, and even more astonished to be offered a column with the magazine a few months later. Sadly, the magazine folded after a couple of years, but by then I was established as writer of many articles in a variety of publications. Be prepared to work for your dreams, and be prepared to step into the limelight if required. Don't be afraid of being noticed.

One of my favorite books is *The Crystal Cave* by Mary Stewart. It's a magical retelling of the Arthurian saga from the point of view of Merlin. In the first chapters he is a young boy in a minor Welsh kingdom; the bastard son of the King's daughter. Nobody knows who his father is. As he tries to forge a future for himself he understands that:

The gods only go with you if you put yourself in their path, and that takes courage.

I completely agree.

Chapter 7

Your Personal Soul Coach

Guardian Angels. Your Personal Soul Coach is waiting for your call!

I was working at an MBS event with a friend some years ago; it was held in a local community center and although it had been busy earlier in the day, it was now very quiet and my friend and I were sat drinking coffee and having a chat. We were discussing the possible existence of angels and had agreed that we both believed that something was out there, but we were unsure of what it actually was... Then we turned to the business of signs from your angels. Now I am upfront about my firm belief that if you need a sign – whatever that form might take – you get a sign; the challenge for us then being to actually notice that sign when it comes. I shall talk about signs in a lot of detail later in this chapter.

The most commonly reported sign is that of a white feather, and as the custodian of five cats, I tend to be a bit skeptical of feathers, as they have a habit of appearing regularly around our home... and are most definitely not angelic signs... However, I do still believe that a white feather can be a sign that an angel has heard you – you just have to be sensible about it! My friend, however, was more dismissive; she thought that it was wishful thinking that a feather could possibly be a sign – after all, they are everywhere: floating on the breeze, on the pavement at our feet and working their way out of our pillows and cushions. She had just finished telling me that I was too gullible when a perfectly formed, snowy white feather slowly floated down between us and landed softly on the table...

Now, we were inside a building, with no soft furnishings from which a feather could suddenly spring, with no open windows and no circulating air conditioning to blow things around.

This beautiful white feather, so fluffy and perfect, seemed to materialize out of nowhere; we both looked up dumbfounded, but there were only the white ceiling tiles far above. It came just at the moment we were discussing it, and it landed squarely between us, challenging us to believe.

Of course we laughed; once we caught our breath we laughed out loud, and some of the other stallholders looked up to see why we were being so noisy. They laughed too, when we told them what had happened... and do you know, that little white feather performed a miracle...

The afternoon had become quiet and sleepy, in the way it sometimes does, when the air is warm and not much is happening, but our laughter seemed to shake up the energy in the room; suddenly we were all more alert and energized. It seems that our energy radiated outwards from the community center, and drew people towards our event; the room filled once more and we all ended the afternoon on a high!

The thing about belief is that it challenges us not to analyze it too much, or it ceases to be. I cannot tell you whether angels exist in the form that we are used to seeing from art: tall humanoid beings, robed in white, with snowy white wings sprouting from between their shoulder blades, but I will tell you that there is something out there, something just out of our field of vision, watching over us and helping us through the twisting path that is life.

I believe in angels.

There are so many stories that call us all the way from the dim and distant past to the present moment of how we have been helped by angels: from Tobias, travelling a rocky road in one of the apocryphal books of the Old Testament, helped along the way by the Archangel Raphael, to the angel who dropped a feather between two friends to support their belief. Originally, there were many more books and stories in the Bible; the apocryphal books are the ones that didn't make it into the final edit.

Every one of us has a Guardian Angel; they are there working in the background for us whether you believe in them or not. But if we work to build a more active connection with them, they can, will and do actively help to change our lives for the better. There is no danger of an angel trying to force his opinion on you, or trying to guide you down the 'wrong' path. Our Guardian Angels have to work within strict boundaries: they cannot 'interfere', they cannot even be proactive unless we invite them to – unless we ask them, and they can only work in a way which is for our highest and best interests. Of course this may not always be what we actually *want* to do, or *want* to make happen, but it will be what we *need*. It's not always the same thing.

How can you discover who they are – and how can you build any sort of a relationship with someone you cannot see or hear? I think it's a bit like having a very powerful form of invisible friend; some of you will have had an invisible playmate when you were a child, so just think of them as having grown up with you – or not – as you choose! There are no rules that say your Guardian Angel cannot be in the form of a child; you can visualize your angel however you wish. I have always had the feeling that they take on whatever form is most appropriate, and possibly even the least likely to scare the living daylights out of us! If I was walking along minding my own business and a burning bush suddenly started talking to me, or a glowing being eight feet tall with giant wings appeared out of nowhere – I would most definitely be screaming and running for my mummy, and so, I suspect, would you too!

It is not in their interest to scare us though, so they stay out of sight for the most part. Although there are those who have the ability to see them in the physical sense, most of us only see them in our dreams and visions, or know they are there because of how they help us.

Think about those times when you have been hoping for

something to go your way – and it does… the job you so wanted, the special person you needed to notice you, the windfall that arrived just in time.

We won the lottery once; I cannot describe the excitement we felt, as no less than five of our numbers were drawn! I was convinced that we must have won a life-changing sum of cash, but it turned out that five numbers on that particular week only meant a payout of £1,400! Still, it was a lot of money and we were both excited about how we were going to spend it… and then, within one week, both of our cars developed serious faults. Can you guess how much the repair bill was? That's right – £1,400… The angels were out there making sure that we could keep our cars on the road; this came at a time when we were seriously broke and if we hadn't had the win, we would have struggled to be able to afford the repairs. I am always, always, thankful when something like this happens… but it would have been nice to have had a little bit left over to play with!

One of the roles of your Guardian Angel is to help you to stay safe, which begs the question, why is there so much hurt in the world? I cannot answer that, nobody can, but I firmly believe that if you believe in a force for good, there has to be an opposite force, a force for evil. The fight between the light and the dark is one that been going on since the dawn of time, and will continue until we are all dust… all each one of us can do is to be aware of the effect of our words and actions on others, and try to be a force for the light, for good. Of course we are only human, which means that there will be times when we fail, but we have to keep trying. Your Guardian Angel will encourage and support you.

There are many ways of beginning the process of building a relationship with your Guardian Angel; you can make it as simple or complicated as you like, but I prefer simple for the reason that I forget what I am supposed to be doing otherwise! If you have to keep referring to a book, or a piece of paper for instructions, then you are less likely to achieve what you want. It is better to be able to do this in a relaxed way, feeling the flow of energy as your spirit lifts. Of course, you may already be talking freely to your angels, but you can still deepen the relationship.

I was first introduced to my Guardian Angels when I was about five years old; I had been suffering dreadful nightmares caused, I believe, by the malignant spirit of a previous occupant of our family home. I was really scared of going to bed and would hide under the covers, not daring to put my head out for fear of what might be out there ready to grab me, but when I eventually fell asleep, the nightmare would take hold and make things worse. I don't like to describe the nightmare even now; it still has the ability to make me feel anxious, even though I have long since broken free of its chains.

In the grip of the dream I would be in the back room of the house, staring outside into the garden... and a woman would be stood beside me, all dressed in blue. Initially, she would be OK, smiling and holding my hand – but then she would change, blackening and charring, and falling in holes in front of me. I would run into the hallway, but the way through the front door would be blocked by a cloud of dense blackness... I would wake up at this point, feeling utterly terrified – but completely unable to tell anyone as I knew I would not be believed.

Then one night, while trapped in the nightmare, I became aware of a ball of golden light in front of me; it was tiny, but growing rapidly, pushing all of the blackness away until I was surrounded by bright white and gold. A man was stood nearby, he came over and took hold of my hand... somehow, I knew that this man was Jesus.

... And yes, I know how completely barking mad that sounds.

Over the years I have gone over this dream many times; it has stayed bright and clear even with the passage of time... the man wearing a creamy-colored robe of a loose woven cloth, sandals on his feet. Shoulder-length hair and amazing brown eyes that were filled with laughter and comfort. I know, of course, that I would have seen him in whatever guise I would have felt most comfortable with; if the dream was something that came entirely from my subconscious, then this is the picture I would have been most familiar with from the children's Bible I owned – except for the eyes. In all the pictures in that book, his eyes were blue, so this was something that I could not have read or seen.

I find it difficult to describe the sense of safety and comfort that came from this man; I was completely at ease, completely calm and confident to be holding his hand. But then he began walking over to two more people that had somehow materialized into the space. Before I come to them, I suppose I should try and describe where I was... It was a place without defined boundaries, without walls, ceiling, roof, or indeed floor – at least as far as I could make out! It was filled with light, at once bright, but soft, no harsh glare to make you shield your eyes, but bright, all the same. The overall color was a sort of golden white; imagine heavenly glowing magnolia and you won't be far off!

Anyway, holding the hand of the man I believed to be Jesus, we walked over to the other two people in the space. There were a man and a woman. They seemed taller than Jesus, but not very tall, bearing in mind that I was only five years old at this time. The man had blue eyes and blond hair and was dressed in a long cream-colored robe. The woman was shorter and was dressed in brown and green. Her dress (if you could call it that) was laced through with leaves, flowers and trailing vines; ivy, bindweed, morning glory. Her hair was the most incredible tangled mess of hazel brown, with twigs, feathers and leaves stuck in seemingly at random. She had the most incredibly green eyes and a mischievous smile...

Jesus took my hand and placed it in the hand of the woman, saying that they would help me to stay safe, to feel the protection that I always had, and that I would be able to ward off the worst of the nightmares, eventually defeating the woman I called the 'Widow Witch'. He also said that his way was not my way –

something that upset me deeply at the time and caused me a lot of heartache over the years as I tried to work out what it meant. As a child, it felt as though I was even being rejected by Jesus – even if I was protected by these other two, it was not a good feeling – but I know now that what he meant was that I was not destined to follow his church, even though I believe in him. Does that sound right? Or do you think I need to call the men in white coats!

It is difficult to talk about this, even so many years after the event; it was a very personal and private dream, experienced at a time when I was terrified every night when I went to bed.

I believe that the man was (and is) my Guardian Angel. His name is Zosi, and he is always there for me; through good times and tough times. I only learned his name a couple of years ago; I had of course been asking for his name since childhood. In my daft ramblings I would go on about it being difficult to keep on referring to a friend as 'my friend' and it was exactly the same thing when referring to a Guardian Angel; I could not keep on saying 'Hello, angel' as I felt silly!

Zosi told me his name over and over again, but I did not hear it… I would go to sleep at night saying, "Please tell me your name!" hoping it would be revealed in a dream, but all that happened was that I would wake up in the middle of the night. I would always awaken at precisely the same time; 12:05 and it took me 20 years to work out that he was trying to tell me his name through the time on the clock… One night, I awoke at the usual time, frustrated because I just wanted to sleep, and as I reached for my drink by the side of the bed, I saw the time reflected in the glass on a photo frame… 12:05 Z0:S1… 'Oh you daft bugger!' I thought. 'It's been there all the time!' From that day to this, I have never woken up at that time… He does still use the time to reassure me though; when I am feeling troubled by something, I will always seem to notice that particular time, day or night. It's nice to feel that he's there… There is more on numbers later in this chapter when I talk about signs in general.

If you have never spoken to your Guardian Angel, then you may well feel a bit daft to start with – but nobody is suggesting you stand in the middle of your local shopping center and shout out, "Oi! Guardian Angel! Where are you?" All you need to do is talk to him in your head… it's a lot easier, much more private and means you can say what is truly in your heart.

Now, if at this stage you are thinking that you really don't believe in angels and are not about to start now, then might I gently suggest that it falls firmly within the category of 'Cannot do any harm, might do some good!' There is absolutely nothing 'bad' that can happen as a result of calling on your Guardian Angel…

I have a dear friend whose three grown-up children live in three different countries, while she lives in a fourth. I asked her how she copes, knowing they are so far away and she said that every time she knows they will be travelling on a plane, for example, she will ask that they are held within the arms of an angel; even if her children are not asking themselves, they will be held safe by the love of their mother and of the angels watching over them.

You can talk to them anywhere of course, but you might like to make a special occasion of it, especially if there is something particular you want to ask, or a topic on which you need guidance. I think of it in the same way that I do when I want to talk over something with a close friend – which is, of course, exactly what you are doing. If you were going out with a friend, you might have lunch, or go shopping, or sit in each other's homes and have coffee and cakes… I will quietly sit somewhere comfortable and, in my head, I will imagine that I am in a celestial coffee shop with Zosi, drinking a heavenly mocha with whipped cream, marshmallows and a Flake (no calories in the heavenly variety!) and chatting about whatever it is that I have on my mind.

In my coffee shop daydream, I get answers to my problems... but they may not be the answers I want to hear! This is because (whether you think the answers come from an angel or just my Inner Voice) the guidance I get will be what I need to move me forwards and will be always in my highest and best interests.

I shall come back to that in a moment, but let's think more about the ideal situation for you to talk to your angels first. You can create a beautiful safe space in your mind which can be whatever you want it to be. It could be a coffee shop, or a woodland glade, a richly tapestried tent in a glowing desert, a beach alongside a blue ocean, or even your own home. It is up to you; whatever you want it to be, it can be. I have various places I go to, depending on my mood and the nature of the chat I need. So the coffee shop serves for the everyday chats, the lighthearted family stuff; there's a peaceful woodland glade, next to a narrow beach, for the 'what should I do with my life' stuff – and for really deep and meaningful spiritual things I have created a circular temple set against the stars, with midnight blue and amethyst cushions and Gregorian chant softly playing in the background... Think about where you feel most comfortable; where you think it would be appropriate for you to talk to your angels... and create it! Over time, you can change it, add to it, move it, do whatever you feel is right and appropriate. The safe space you create at 17 will probably be very different from the one you create at 50. There are no rules except the ones you create yourself.

The next thing is to consider how you begin... when teaching meditation, some students have said that they have created their space... sat and waited in it, but nobody turned up! This is actually quite common and completely normal, especially when you are just starting out, and especially if you feel a little silly sitting there imagining meeting an angel in a coffee shop! I have also discovered that starting out with the belief that nothing will happen generally means that well... nothing will happen! You need to approach the exercise with an open heart and mind, and accept that it may not happen on your first attempt… in the same way that your blind date might not turn up first time either!

If this approach really does not seem to be working for you, then there are many other ways of meeting and beginning the process of working with your Guardian Angel. The 'Active Meditation' approach described in Chapter 3 might be the way forward for you; I use this in addition to the other methods described here. These days I find it easy to talk to angels wherever I am and whatever I am doing, but it was not always the case – especially when I was a teenager, with all the teenage angst! Look for the gaps in your day: times when you might be dealing with the laundry, walking from the car into work, sitting on the bus, putting on your makeup – any moments when you are busy with something that gives you a reason to be where you are, doing what you are doing, and in your mind, you can carry on a conversation with your Guardian Angel. The important thing is to try – but try with an open mind and an open heart.

Once you have opened the lines of communication in some way, then you can try something else… and generally that will be asking for a sign that they have actually heard you and all this talking in your mind is not just the product of a feverish imagination.

It's a sign!

From a white feather to the same numbers turning up everywhere, songs, pictures, cloud formations… even a spider crawling up your arm just might be a sign… but how do you know which is a sign and which is just wishful thinking?

It is, of course, deeply personal; what might be a sign of absolute proof to me might be complete and utter rubbish to you! The key to signs is that they are there right when you need them. The most commonly asked for sign is that the angels have heard you, that they really are out there, listening to your desperate babbling… I sometimes wonder what they must think of us as, always on at them for signs, signs, signs; we must seem like small children pestering mum for an ice cream sometimes!

If you ask for your sign and something happens more or less straight away, then yes, absolutely, that is a sign… if on the other hand you ask, and then don't notice a sign for another three days, well, that is probably not a sign – at least not the one you were looking for. They always hear us, they always answer us, but we don't always hear their voice.

I have a little fault on my car; it doesn't happen very often, but is annoying when it does. Every now and again, when I turn on the ignition, the radio doesn't come on… and then at some point during the journey, it will spring into life at a completely random moment…

One morning, I left for work, and the radio did not come on. On this particular morning, I was feeling a bit down – I can't even remember why now (that's how important it was), but not having a radio in the car to sing along to was not helping my mood. I was driving along and talking out loud to my Guardian Angel at the same time about whatever was going on in my life – and at one point I asked, out loud, for a definite, no nonsense sign that someone was actually listening to my ramblings…

… At which moment the radio sprang into life, as Aretha Franklin sang the line, "I say a little prayer for you…"! I laughed out loud and my mood lifted immediately as I carried on driving. This just had to be a cast iron sign – the timing of it and the line from the song were pretty definite. However, by the time I had reached my parking spot, I had begun to feel it was all in my head again, so in a somewhat shamefaced manner, I found myself walking down the path towards the center of town asking for yet another sign! This time I was muttering under my breath saying that I was really grateful for the first sign, and yes, it was fairly unmissable, but could I have another please… just to be sure? Even as I was saying it I was wondering if angels ever get frustrated with us!

This time, I had barely finished muttering when I turned a corner and walked straight into a little white feather, perfectly formed, hanging from a gossamer thread, at eye level! This path is quite busy and someone else had been walking a short distance ahead of me, so either they had somehow missed it... which is difficult to believe because it was right in the middle of the path, or it was waiting for me.

Needless to say, I was astonished and began burbling thanks out loud – which caused the elderly couple coming the other way to give me an alarmed stare and a wide berth! I was grinning though; it made my day to think I had had two signs, right when I asked.

We all have times when we feel down and just need to feel that someone is there for us, so don't feel awkward about asking your Guardian Angel to let you know that he is around. Here are some other examples of signs.

Numbers

Angels seem to have an affinity with numbers; many people say they have seen the same single number or series of numbers over and over again. Probably the most commonly reported instance of this is waking up and looking at the clock at precisely the same time night after night; remember, this is actually how I eventually worked out the name of my Guardian Angel. I had a phase of waking up at 12.05am. I couldn't understand it – I would drop off naturally at around 11.00–11.30pm and then wake up with a start just after midnight! This went on for about three weeks until I eventually connected it to my work on trying to discover the name of my Guardian Angel. The numbers were reflected on a glass on the bedside table; 12:05 turns into Zosi, and I had my name. I cannot prove it, of course I can't, but it felt right – and taking note of your feelings, what you know instinctively to be true, is crucial to any form of spiritual development.

Do you have a 'Lucky Number'? Most of us have a number

which has a significance or meaning; it can be related to anything or nothing, it just 'feels' right to you – and you notice when it comes up.

My lucky number has always been 8; I don't know how it started, it just felt right. When I discovered Numerology, I also found that my numbers are also 8; the number of my name, the number of my date of birth and many others besides.

There are lots of books and resources out there on Numerology. I'm not going to go into it in any detail here, but if you want to discover your personal numbers then this is how you do it.

For dates: Simply add all the individual digits together until you reach a single number e.g. 13.01.2013 would be 1+3+0+1+2+0+1+3 = 11. 11 then becomes 1+1=2 – the number would be 2.

For letters: Each letter has its own number relevant to its place in the alphabet e.g. A=1, B=2, C=3. You would work out the numbers for the word of phrase and then add them together in the same way as above until you reach a single digit.

Each number has a meaning in Numerology, but for those you will need to look them up elsewhere!

Whether it has anything to do with Numerology or not, my number 8 has followed me all my life. From license plates to winning raffle tickets and lottery numbers and the number of our home, it seems that if it's going to be good for me, the number 8 will be in there somewhere!

Images

Just as numbers can pop up all over the place, so images may be repeated too. If you are asking for the courage to speak out on something, for example, you may find that you notice things related to lions, tigers and other big cats! The Archangel Ariel is very much associated with helping us when we need that extra shot of courage; his symbol is the lion, which can be extended to other members of the cat family...

The accepted associations for angels e.g. Ariel – Courage, Gabriel – Communication, Michael – protection etc. are only a tiny part of the story, however; there will be occasions when you will feel that you have been helped by an angel – and it won't be something that falls within that 'accepted' association. Some years ago, we visited Truro while on holiday in Cornwall (we go every year, absolutely love it there), and I was looking for a particular book on angels I had read about online. I knew there was a Waterstones in town, but we just couldn't find it (this was before we all had mobile Internet!), so we drove around the one-way system for ages trying to see it before we parked, completely without success! Eventually we parked up in a car park about 50 miles from the city center (well, it felt like it!) and walked back in. By now I was completely fed up and on the point of giving up, but I decided to have one last go and sent up a request to any angels who might be listening to guide me in the right direction.

Almost immediately, I spotted a van advertising Sky TV; it was covered with a huge image of a lion. It passed us going in the opposite direction, but I thought we might as well follow it; we had no idea where we were going, so this was as good as any method of finding our way! We hadn't gone very far, when I noticed a car with the number plate that included L 1 O N... I cannot remember it exactly now, but the word 'Lion' really stood out for me, so we followed that for a couple more minutes. By now we were in a very open area of the city. It was bustling with people, but over the hubbub, I could just about make out a song; it was *The Circle of Life* from *The Lion King*! We fought our way through the shoppers towards the sound; it was coming from a branch of HMV – and right next door... was Waterstones! They had the book I wanted (*A Dictionary of Angels* by Gustav Davidson), and a couple more besides. Every single time I pick up that book, it makes me smile to think of how we were guided to the right place by lions!

The images that angels use to make you sit up and take notice might fall within those accepted associations, but it might not. It depends on the circumstances, what has relevance and meaning for you – and what there is around that can be manipulated into a sign, which brings me to the next thing...

Clouds

I love clouds; we have an ever-changing scene above our heads – think how utterly boring it would be if there were no clouds! Here in the UK, we are blessed (!) with constantly changing weather (someone once said to me that every other country on the planet has a climate, but we just have 'weather'!) that provides us with clouds of just about every type. Clouds can form into an infinite variety of shapes and images, and just occasionally, these images feel like personal and private signs, just for us. I have experienced so many beautiful signs in the form of clouds – but you do have to remember that they need to be there at the right time, in order for you to say that yes, that was definitely a sign.

Thanks to mobile phone photography, I have managed to record some of the amazing cloud formations that have felt to me like signs, from the giant 'X' in the sky formed by crossing contrails (I badly needed a sort of angelic hug that day; this was right in front of me as I got in my car and looked up through the windshield), to glowing angelic 'figures' seemingly hovering high above, and even a giant, perfectly-formed cloud feather over Portsmouth. If you want to see these, and other pictures, please visit my website and follow the link to my Blog. You can also upload your own angelic cloud signs!

Dreams

When we sleep, the 'ego mind', that part of us that manages all the day to day stuff, also sleeps. Our subconscious mind can become more active and, as we enter REM sleep, we dream...

All of us dream, even if you are one of those who finds it a challenge to remember your dreams. I believe that it is much easier for guides, guardians and angels – as well as our loved ones in spirit – to communicate with us through our dreams. When we are awake, we are constantly analyzing what we hear and see, as well as keeping up a constant internal chatter. It must be like trying to tune into a local radio station through immense static (or like trying to find Radio Luxembourg when I was a teenager!). When all that is shut down, when we are dreaming, it can be easier to find a way through. Of course, once they have found that way through, we then have to remember the dream in order to be able to benefit and understand.

Many of us will have experienced dreams of our loved ones – especially in the first few months after they have passed into spirit, and it can provide real comfort to those left behind. The dreams can be exceptionally vivid and stay with you for a long time.

A couple of weeks before my godmother Hilda passed away, I had an incredible dream. I was at a party in a village hall somewhere. I don't know exactly when it was, but the music was of the late 1940s, or early 1950s, played by a band on the stage. The women were beautifully dressed, the men dashing, with many in uniform… and in among them all was a young woman that I knew was my godmother. Suddenly there was the sound of a car horn outside, and the music stopped. We all went out to see what was happening; there was a young man outside in an open-topped car, he disembarked and came around to where we were all stood. With a beaming smile, he held out his hand… and a blushing Hilda stepped forward. Without uttering a word he led her to the car and opened the passenger door. She got in the car, never once taking her eyes from his face. He closed the door, went around to the driver's side, got back in, started the engine and drove away… Everyone applauded and cheered and then went back to the party in the hall… the dream faded…

My Aunt Hilda was married to Reuben, who had himself passed a few years previously. She had developed Parkinson's disease in her later years, which had had a devastating effect on her mobility and ability to use her hands. I firmly believe that my dream showed how Reuben was waiting for her, and when I heard that she had died, I knew that they were now reunited in spirit, forever young. I felt very privileged to have had this dream and it will stay with me forever.

Of course other dreams will not become apparent as signs or messages for some time and most may just be a mishmash of the day's events, recycled and turned into what seems like nonsense! I have often said that when I write my autobiography (if!), it will be called "Shopping for Curtains with Jean-Luc Picard" after an incredibly vivid dream in which I found myself in the Net Curtain section of a local department store, accompanied by the entire bridge crew of the *Next Generation* Enterprise, phasers set to stun – and no, I have absolutely no idea what that was all about!

Music

The melodies and lyrics of music have the ability to affect us at a very deep level; hearing a particular song can whisk us back in our hearts to a special time, place or someone… Sometimes this is all it takes, a snatch of melody to remind us that we are watched over and protected, something to make us smile, or tug at our emotions; sometimes it's the actual lyrics within a song that bring us a direct message. Angels are not there at the radio stations, making sure the playlist is in the right order – but they can affect our consciousness and attention, so that we really notice the songs, at the right time.

There are also cases where an individual has heard what seems to be a heavenly choir coming from somewhere… but they have been unable to find a source for it. This is very rare, and seems to happen mostly in cases of extreme stress or anxiety.

The Tiny Signs

Most of the signs we receive will be tiny signs, things we really have to watch out for, things that can be very easy to miss, or which pass us by in a second, before vanishing forever. I cannot give you a list of these, they are very personal, the sort of thing that only you will recognize as a sign. One of my own favorites happened while walking around a lake with some of our friends in Finland in summer 2012. I had managed to fall over twice that day, once while being helped down a set of steps and then again while walking around this lake. I am not exactly steady on my feet at the best of times, but twice in one day was a bit ridiculous and I asked for a reassurance that I would manage to stay upright for the rest of our day out. A couple of minutes later I decided to take some photos of the patterns of lichen on a large boulder to try out the macro lens on my camera – and lo! There was the teeniest tiniest perfectly shaped heart on the rock, formed from delicate lichen. It's incredibly beautiful, and I felt that it was a sign meant just for me. I did manage to reach the end of the walk without further incident, you will be relieved to hear.

Manifestation

This is just about the most unlikely thing to happen; I often wonder how I might react if an angel manifested in front of me, as I said earlier. Somehow I cannot imagine accepting it meekly... I think I would be terrified, at least initially!

Having said that, I believe that I have experienced an angelic manifestation; this is how it happened.

As related elsewhere in this book, I have had breast cancer. The diagnosis came at the end of 2004, chemotherapy and surgery followed, and by the time I reached the end of June 2005, I hoped I was through the worst of it and on the road to recovery at last.

The treatment had been tough, but at no time did I ever sense that my life was in danger; it might sound strange, but I trusted in my medical and surgical teams – and had complete faith in God and the angels and whoever else was up there to pull me through. The only thing worrying me was that I didn't seem to be 'sensing' or 'feeling' anything through my intuition or psychic senses. It was almost as though the main switch had been thrown into the 'off' position as the treatment had progressed. I felt bereft, abandoned, just when I needed the support the most. I now believe that it could be a sort of safety valve, designed to protect you when you are at your lowest, perhaps combined with extreme fatigue and the effect of the various drugs thrown at me during this period.

After my mastectomy and reconstruction in April 2012, I had developed that serious infection on the reconstruction. I had to go back into the hospital, have blood transfusions, have the wound underneath reopened and left open, with a drain to draw out the ghastly infective material. It's not nice to discuss and was an absolutely awful and debilitating period, probably the worst month of my life. I came out of the hospital with the drain still in place in the open wound. It had to be dressed daily by a nurse and stunk to high heaven; the dressings covered me from waist to shoulder almost, from the center of my chest to the middle of my back. I felt about a hundred years old and was seriously depressed and tired during this time. Eventually, in mid June, I went back in for further surgery; my surgeon (an angel in his own right and official miracle worker) cut away the dead tissue and closed up the wound. I went home a couple of days later and immediately began to feel better…

One night towards the end of June, Phil and I retired to bed as usual and went to sleep. I awoke with a start a couple of hours later and opened my eyes; I was facing the wall and, to my surprise, there appeared to be two glowing objects floating in front of me… I wasn't that concerned though; I thought it was a trick of the light, so I lay there and stared at them for a bit, but after a few minutes, I began to wonder exactly how this 'trick of the light' was formed.

We always sleep with the curtains open a bit; as we are at the front of the house there is a net curtain which filters the light from the streetlamp outside and there is a tree near the streetlamp which could affect the light too. I got out of bed and went over to the window, twiddled the curtains, waved my arms in front of the light coming through the gap, but it didn't appear to change anything. I went back over to the wall and had a look at the glowing objects, they almost looked like heads... This was ridiculous, I must be still dreaming! I nipped across the hall to the loo, put the light on, used the facilities, washed my hands and splashed cold water on my face. I was definitely awake.

I returned to our bedroom; they were still there. OK, what on earth were they; I walked over, sat on the edge of the bed and had a really good look. Each object was slightly smaller than a football, a gently glowing orb of golden light; the surface was moving, almost rippling, and I could detect what appeared to be facial features, eyes, nose, lips moving as if it was speaking... Beneath the main orb were a mass of slowly moving, weaving strands of light, looking for all the world like the tendrils of a jellyfish. One of the orbs was slightly higher than the other – and they were most definitely three-dimensional, which meant that they surely could not be a trick of the light, could they?

I should have felt scared, but I wasn't; I should have been waking Phil up, but curiously I didn't feel I needed to. I felt quite calm – and reassured even, that these strange objects were no threat. I watched them for quite a while, I couldn't tell you for exactly how long; but eventually I decided to get back into bed. As I dropped off to sleep, they still hovered, gently glowing...

In the morning, I dismissed it. It was a dream, it was a trick of the light, it could not possibly be anything even remotely 'weird'. Still, when I went to bed that night, I remembered to ask for some clarification, please; another appearance even! Nothing happened. I awoke the following morning from a deep and refreshing sleep – but nothing.

More nothing happened the following night as well; so on the third night, I just went to sleep...

... and awoke a couple of hours later with a start!

I immediately looked over to the wall, but all I could see was the light filtering through the curtains. I got up and nipped to the loo, as you do, and it was not until I returned that I noticed the two glowing heads had returned, but they were not by the wall... This time, they were floating directly above my pillow!

This threw me a bit; if they were a trick of the light, then surely it could only appear in the same spot? The wall above my head was not illuminated by anything; it was in deep shadow, so how could there be anything glowing against it. Once again, I stood and examined the objects; I cannot be sure of course, but they certainly looked like the same objects that had appeared previously. Cautiously I got back into bed and lay on my back, looking up at them. The movement from the tendrils of light was hypnotic and I quickly fell asleep.

I have not seen them since. I cannot tell you with any degree of certainty what they were... but I believe that they were angelic. There you go, I've said it; I believe that I saw two floating angel... erm... heads. Honest.

I'm not that bonkers (honest); I consider myself to be a skeptical believer in the paranormal: which is that I will look for all other rational explanations before considering that something might just be otherworldly. I know that I was awake; I know that it could not possibly have been caused by a light effect. What does that leave?

The fact that at no time did I feel even faintly scared or anxious has led me to conclude that there was no harm in whatever they were... and the clincher, for me, was that following these two incidents I recovered my sense of intuition, my feeling of connection to God and the angels; I no longer felt alone. Even better, was that everything felt better, sharper, stronger; if I had been on dial-up before, now I was definitely running on broadband!

The friend who will never fail you.
I have to repeat myself here: it really doesn't matter whether or not you believe in your Guardian Angel; he will still believe in you. I get quite a few letters and e-mails from people who say that they are convinced that they have no Guardian Angel, or that they have called out to them on countless occasions and not been answered – "Why is my Guardian Angel ignoring me?" they ask me.

The answer is very simple. Yes, you most definitely have a Guardian Angel and no he or she is most definitely not ignoring you.

If you ask, you will receive an answer; but if it is not the answer you wanted, are you prepared to accept it? In my chapter on your Inner Voice, I shall show you how to listen for those answers, how to check the truth of what you hear and how to be positive about every answer. Your Guardian Angel is looking over your shoulder right now as you read this, and he's probably shaking his head in exasperation over the number of carefully laid signs that you missed, whispered answers that you didn't hear and dream encounters that melted away with the morning sun.

The first step as always is an open heart and mind, the rest will follow.

I am sometimes asked if your loved ones in spirit can act as your Guardian Angels and, although it may seem or feel as though they do, I don't believe they are actual angels. I believe that our Guardian Angels are assigned before we are born and stay with us throughout our lives, and then we also have different guides who come and go depending on what's happening in our lives. Our loved ones in spirit may act as guides, depending on what we need right then. When I was experiencing the nagging shoulder pain that was eventually diagnosed as breast cancer, I believe it was my Big Grandma who was watching over me and nagging me to go to the doctor. After I finally mentioned the shoulder pain to my GP in passing after a year of niggling twinges – it mysteriously vanished, Big Grandma had done her job and made me sit up and take notice.

In 1989, I lost a dear friend of mine in a motorcycle accident. It happened on a beautiful Sunday evening in July, but I didn't discover it until Tuesday. I drove into Portsmouth to work that Tuesday morning, and parked my car in a quiet side street, before walking to the office. It is a walk I will never forget; I had only gone a few steps when I thought I heard my name being called. I turned, but there was nobody there. I continued walking, but now I had the strangest sensation that my friend was walking just behind me; I stopped, and turned, but again, there was nobody there. It continued so strongly, that after a couple of minutes, I stopped and turned round and called out for him to come out from wherever he was hiding! Silence. I finished my walk into work feeling distinctly odd. At lunchtime, one of my colleagues went out for the local paper; I glanced at it as I walked by his desk – and my blood ran cold. My friend's face filled the front page and the headline screamed the awful news at me. I couldn't talk to anyone about it; I turned it all inwards, the shock was so deep. Over the next three weeks, it all became a little strange; I could smell his aftershave, the towels in the bathroom were being moved around; it felt as though he was physically there, just out of sight. At first it was a comfort, then it became oppressive, and in the end I remember shouting into the empty air for him to leave me alone. I cannot tell you how guilty I felt when it all stopped, instantly, from that moment. I had deserted him when he needed me.

So now fast forward to 1998, and the football World Cup. Phil was working away from home, I was watching the footie while sat on the floor in the living room; the kids were in bed, England had drawn 2–2 with Argentina and the dreaded penalty shoot-out was about to begin. As I sat there in the semi-darkness, I began to sense someone sat behind me; nothing scary, even though I knew I was alone apart from the sleeping children upstairs. As the penalties progressed to their inevitable doom for England, I knew who it was, sat there with me, so I talked to him and said sorry for sending him away nine years previously. I felt that although I had agonized over it for years, it had never been an issue for him; he was at peace and that was all that mattered.

Both of these incidents built on my already unshakeable belief in an afterlife, but then outside proof came from a chance meeting. I had been halfheartedly thinking about having a reading with a medium, when my best friend Tracey told me about this chap she had heard of who lived in Bristol. He sounded really good, so I called to make an appointment, only to be told that he was fully booked for at least a year ahead. There was someone else they could recommend though, a lady who also lived in Bristol. I called and made an appointment, and Tracey and I drove the hundred miles across country a few days later.

As we walked in through the door, she looked me in the eye and said, "I see you've brought a young man with you; he passed a good few years ago now, but he knows how bad you felt, and he was talking to you during the football!"

Now, you could guess some stuff, but not before I walked in, and certainly, absolutely not about the football. I had not told anyone about that – after all, would you confess to having a chat with a dead friend while watching England lose on penalties? There was more, much more, including an astounding comment that the spirit world referred to my lovely husband Phil as the Potato Man because of his love of spuds in any form! Sadly she has also now passed into spirit; I know she will be watching over her loved ones.

He watched over me for years, I know that; but as I grew

spiritually, so I did not need that close contact, and he was able to leave me to my own devices. It's a good thing. I don't believe it's fair on our loved ones to try and hold on to them when they pass; they have to move on, and we will of course meet them again, when our time comes.

Spirit Guides are just that, individuals to guide your spirit through your life. Through personal development, spiritual awakening, growing up, life-changing illness and recovery, and eventually, through the change to a life after life.

I'm not afraid of death, although the method of dying concerns me a little, which I think is entirely reasonable. When my friend died, it was a severe shock; he had not reached 30 and had just got engaged. We were expecting to be able to take the mick out of each other for decades to come, but he is at peace. Death can be a happy thing; when my Little Grandma passed on in 2012, it was a blessed release from a life which had ceased to give her happiness. Age and infirmity had taken her away from her beloved garden, from feeling the sun and wind on her face and it was her time to make the journey back into sunshine.

Our job here on earth is to keep our loved ones alive in our memories; the Mexicans have a tradition that we die three 'deaths'.

The first is when our body physically dies. The second is when we hold the funeral and release the spirit. The third and final death comes when there is nobody left who remembers us.

May you live forever in the memories of those who love you.

Chapter 8

The What If Factor

How do you cope when life throws something at you?

Life is full of events that seem intent on diverting us from the path we want to follow: from the tiny distractions of the everyday, to the huge things, the things that stop us in our tracks and put everything on pause.

Here are a couple of examples to make you think about how you cope with change – and let's face it, life is all about change.

I like to have at least a rough idea of what I would like to do, or have to do, each day. The days when I have fixed commitments, such as going out to work, are a lot easier than those when I am attempting to work from home, so let's examine what can happen when I work from home.

The alarm goes off at 7.30am: I have a choice of getting up, or staying in bed for an extra half hour... or hour. If I get up, I feel energized, confident about the day ahead; if I lay in bed for that extra half hour, I might feel a little guilty and that can carry through the day. It's tempting to think that the whole day has gone to pot just because it started in a way I hadn't planned.

If I do get up on time, sometimes I don't even make it downstairs before something hurls itself firmly in my path, determined to throw me off course! The kids may be grown-up, but they still rely on mum to sort their lives out for them, from dressing minor injuries, making appointments and filling out forms, to feeding them and doing their washing – and strangely enough, most of this seems to need doing just when I am trying to wake up! I like to wake up gradually, with the radio coming on about half an hour before I need to stagger out of bed, as opposed to going from deep sleep to full consciousness in a nanosecond because a teenager has just burst into my bedroom with a sheet of paper and a pen for a note which needs writing NOW! Anyone who has children will also be familiar with the feeling of creeping horror that something, or someone, is watching you as you lay drowsing in bad with your eyes closed. Opening your eyes a fraction to see a shape looming over you in the semi-darkness is guaranteed to make your heart leap into your throat and give you a case of the screaming abdabs! Realizing that it is one of your offspring does nothing to calm the frantic pounding in your chest!

However, on this mythically calm morning, I make it all the way downstairs to the kitchen, the kettle and coffee without interruption. (Completely unrealistic of course!)

I even manage to eat my breakfast as soon as it is made...

I used to set myself up for failure nearly every day. On the days that I work from home, the plan was to be sat at my desk by 9.00am. However, on most days that I work from home, I am lucky to be sat at my desk by 11.30...

One of the cats will have thrown up, or brought in some wildlife which will need catching and releasing, or taking to the wildlife sanctuary for treatment, the washing will need sorting out, dinner for the evening will need planning (why is it that nobody except mum can ever make a decision on what to have for dinner?), bins need emptying, post needs dealing with... and a thousand and one other little everyday events to distract you from getting on with what you want to.

Dealing with minor daily events sometimes just requires you to rethink how you plan your day; rather than attempting to sit down by 9.00am, give yourself an extra hour (or two) to sort out the domestic stuff. Beating yourself up because you cannot achieve what may be an unrealistic target gets you nowhere except down; down, down, dooby doo down, grotty and grumpy to be precise.

The temptation is to just throw the whole day in the bin... which makes you beat yourself up even more and can lead to self-

sabotaging behavior, which in my case means eating lots of biscuits and chocolate!

Some days I feel a bit like a housefly, moving randomly in circles… I start out well, going downstairs to feed the kitties and put the washing on before going for my shower; and then once dried and dressed, I go back down for my essential first cup of coffee, start opening the post, see something that needs my attention and make the necessary call, then the washing machine finishes. I empty it and hang out the laundry, but a deliveryman rings the doorbell before I finish it, I leave the washing for a moment to open the package but while I am struggling to get the tape off a friend calls me for a chat. Twenty minutes later and my coffee is cold; I make a fresh one and the door goes again – this time it's my friend Lynn with my Avon order. We chat for a while and my coffee goes cold again; this time I zap it and drink it while scanning a magazine for inspiration on what to have for dinner. Quick check on what I need to buy, and make a list. At this point I notice the ghastly smell drifting in from the hallway and get some bags out to deal with the cat litter; the bin appears to be overflowing (why is it that only mums notice when a bin needs emptying?), so I sort that out… and clean off the bin lid while I'm at it (teenagers seem to find it tricky to ensure that rubbish goes into the bin and not all over it!). I glance at the clock and realize I need to get moving if the urgent parcel I need to post is going to arrive tomorrow, so I dig out the tape and brown paper and wrap it up, then dash off in the car, forgetting my list of essentials for tonight's dinner – never mind, I can sort of remember what I needed and buy that. While out, I take a call from the school to say my daughter has torn her toenail badly, so I call the surgery and make an appointment for the nurse to dress it… collect daughter and go home to scene of devastation. The kitchen is covered with half-opened post, torn packaging, Avon sunscreen bottles, scattered pegs and damp washing. There is a bin bag on the floor next to a dripping bin lid. My half-drunk

coffee is on the draining board next to my shopping list and a soggy magazine.

I have forgotten two of the essential ingredients for the evening meal, so it looks like we'll be having one of my make-it-up-as-I-go-along mystery meals again!

… And by now it's 1.00pm and it feels as though the day has completely got away from me yet again…

At this point I have a choice to make; I can throw my hands up in the air and throw a hissy fit, complain that the day has gone to hell in a handcart and I might as well give up. This will probably put me in a thoroughly bad mood and I might be snappy with everyone else in the house. My bad mood will almost definitely rub off on them and we might all end the day feeling down and depressed.

On the other hand, I could take a deep breath, finish the washing, clear up the mess and find a recipe that I do have the ingredients for. Oh – and make myself another coffee, and some lunch and actually sit down to eat it!

In other words, accept it and move on! This sort of thing is going to happen every single day of your life; do you really want to let it stop you from enjoying your days?

We all know folks who do exactly that; seeming to suffer from a never ending stream of minor catastrophes, always complaining about their lot in life. Some people don't seem to be happy unless they have a disaster to moan about!

My husband used to work in London; we don't live near a railway station and his hours were very unsociable so the only way of commuting was by road.

He would come in every night and give me a blow by blow account of the traffic conditions and how many near misses and terrible driving incidents he had either witnessed or experienced; some of which had happened on his way into work between 4.00 and 6.00am and which he had stewed upon all day.

I argued that by doing this he was giving the other driver the

power to ruin his day. He has allowed a minor incident of poor judgement by someone else on their way to London, something that perhaps barely registers for that driver, to color and affect his mood and behavior. On the other hand, he could acknowledge it at the time, accept that it had happened, and move on. End of story.

The way in which we approach the distractions of the day can and does affect our ability to succeed in life.

We cannot stop all these things happening, this is real life; but we can change the way in which we approach them and deal with them. These days, I do most of my writing in the afternoon and evening; it helps me to plan my time more effectively. I get more done and I feel better about myself.

There are times, however, that are always going to divert you, at least for a while. Towards the end of 2011, my life turned upside down because of family illness. My father had been seriously ill for years, in and out of the hospital and then into respite care. Late one night in December, I had a call from my stepmum to say that he had been admitted to the hospital from the nursing home and was critically ill. I picked her up in my car, and we drove to the hospital where we were led into the relatives' room to wait. Years of watching medical dramas have left me with a somewhat understandable fear of the relatives' room, and when the doctor came to talk to us, it was to say that Dad was slipping away. I called my brothers and we sat with him almost around the clock for nearly four days until he peacefully passed away. While this was going on, my grandma, who was then 93, fell backwards down the stairs... she cracked her head and her ribs and the shock brought on aggressive senile dementia. She was admitted to the hospital, was transferred to a nursing home and within a few short months had gone, leaving us bereft.

These sorts of events, while completely natural, are always going to affect you and you should never feel guilty for not being able to continue as usual. There are no rules for grief; everyone feels it in their own way and at their own pace.

I had a difficult relationship with my father; my feelings for him were based on frustration and some resentment for the way he treated us as children. He was a bit of a cold fish emotionally, and an absolute miser financially; my younger brothers had a much better experience of him after our parents divorced.

My grandma was a very different personality; she had a tough life, but was happy to share whatever she had with us. By her own admission, she was the "Easiest person in the world to live with" (!), something which was absolutely not true – I lived with her at three different times and she was excessively house-proud and fastidious, with standards I find it completely hopeless to emulate; she happened to notice that my oven door was covered in fat splatters a couple of years ago (still is, come to that!) and said that she didn't know how I could sleep at night, knowing that the oven door was dirty!

She may have been less than five feet tall, but she was a strong woman, worked well into her 70s, who never owed a penny to anyone in her life, and we all loved her to bits. My mum and stepdad bought into her house in the 1990s as they wanted to make sure she was looked after. She steadfastly refused to accept that age can reduce our capabilities... we caught her up a ladder painting the gable end of the house when she was in her mid 70s... Even when she was in her late 80s she was still gardening, still cleaning anything not nailed down and still telling my long-suffering mum "Wait until I'm gone, then you'll know, mark my words!" I would help to keep an eye on her when my parents were on holiday; she would take this as an opportunity to do all the things we thought might be beyond her years, such as hand washing the enormous floor-to-ceiling curtains from the vast windows in the back room. She had them made to measure in the 1960s; they are about 10 feet long and each curtain is more than 6 feet wide, they are immensely heavy and positively hazardous to take down and put up. I'm sure that she was up that ladder the second the taxi had vanished taking Mum and Rob to the airport! I hope I'm as bloody-minded when I'm an octogenarian, but maybe a little more aware of my limitations too.

My grief for my dad and grandma flow along completely different lines, but there was one subject on which we all came together, and that was gardening. Grandma had grown up in Locks Heath, near Southampton, in a house with a large plot of land that her father worked, in addition to being employed as a postman. He grew everything from kitchen produce to fruit in orchards; but for the young Frances, the jewel in the crown was the hosts of golden daffodils that bloomed in the spring which he would sell to the local florists and gypsies for resale in Fareham, Southampton and the villages around.

My dad Ron, on the other hand, came to growing things later in life, but it gave him a lot of pleasure to talk about his garden. With both of them, I could wander around the garden, pointing out flowers and fruit, discussing the best way of slug disposal and generally passing a happy half hour.

Working in a garden, planting seeds and watching them grow is a deeply spiritual experience and helps us to come to terms with the essential cycles of birth, growth and death. I have a large bay tree in a ridiculously huge pot in my little courtyard next to my kitchen. When I bought it, at a local garden center in 1994, it was two leaves on a twig; we've been through a lot together, me and that bay tree, but we're both still here…

During and after those times of illness and death, I found it difficult to write anything. My mind was crowded full of memories, some good, some – not so good… but I understood that this was a natural process. Of course I felt guilty sometimes, I love writing and want to share my thoughts; but equally I know that there will always be times when my attention is needed elsewhere. I needed that time to reflect and grieve, as you will, when your loved ones slip quietly away from you.

The actual time this takes is up to you, there are no rules…

but when the time comes to take up the reins of life fully once more, do it with a smile on you face, and in your heart. Your loved ones will always live on in your hearts.

Acknowledge, accept, move on.

The list of things that will try to stop you from achieving what you want on a daily, weekly, monthly or lifetime basis is unending. The time has come now to discuss how we can actually get anything done!

The first key is not to overload yourself with too much. I split things into three main categories to help me prioritize:

1. Firm commitments.
2. Things I *have* to do, but which I can move around, or get help with.
3. Stuff I *want* to do.

I have a *firm commitment* to be at work at a certain time or produce work by a certain time, and everything else has to work around that. I may have to attend appointments with doctors and dentists, but they also have to fit in with work. When the kids were younger, I had a firm commitment to the school runs and this meant that I had to fit work around that. My firm commitments take up nearly half of my waking hours.

I *have* to look after everyone at home: washing, housework, cooking, counseling, refereeing, homework (apparently), shopping and nursing, along with a million other essential tasks that form family life. I can move the tasks around though, they may need doing, but not necessarily *now*, or by me; Phil is brilliant, he does more than his share and the kids muck in if we ask them. I've had to accept that maybe they are not going to volunteer, but need a bit of gentle prodding! I have to do weekly admin tasks for my business and have to schedule enough time for this. It's really easy to stretch all of this over every other waking hour I have, leaving absolutely no time for me at all, so this is where I have to decide what is essential right now, and what I can delegate, or leave for the time being. As I am writing this, the washing machine has just played a cheery little tune to tell me that it has finished; I have to sort this out now, or the school uniform won't be dry for tomorrow morning. I can't delegate this task as I am completely obsessive about my washing! I find sorting out the washing therapeutic in a weird sort of way; I like to make sure that it dries in such a way that it never needs ironing. I don't believe in ironing unless it's unavoidable. With a family of five, I would have spent most of my life ironing! If they want something ironed, they know where the ironing board is. We visited the Ideal Home Show in London a few years ago; there was a company demonstrating a device that claimed to wash, dry and iron your clothes, saving you a whole week out of every year that you would not spend ironing. I told the man on the stand that it wouldn't save me any time all, as I don't iron anyway! It's fine if you love your ironing, we are all different, and that's as it should be.

Later today, I have to cook dinner, but the time can be moved around. Tomorrow morning when the post arrives, I can either stop what I am doing, or leave it to one side and finish off one task before starting on something else. Planning your day may involve a list of many small tasks, or just one or two. The important thing is to try to prioritize, so that by the time you go to bed you feel comfortable that you achieved what you wanted; but it's just as important that if things don't go to plan you accept it and move on without beating yourself up or feeling guilty. Tomorrow is a new day.

I *want* to read lots of books, go to the footie with Phil, spend time in my garden, spend quality time with my friends and family and cook for pleasure instead of necessity. I don't think this is unreasonable.

Try this exercise for yourself, working out where your priorities lie.

There's a magic word that I discovered quite by chance that can really help you to find more time for yourself, a calmer and more relaxed way of life and the ability to sleep without feeling utterly drained and exhausted.

It's only a short little word – are you ready for this? I promise you it's going to change everything for the better…

This is it then.

No.

No… That's it; not yes, no.

A very short word, just two letters, that can have a huge and lasting impact. Here's an example to show you what I mean.

"Mum, can I go to the cinema tonight?"

"How are you getting there and back?"

"Can you give us a lift please?"

"I'd love to normally, but I have to be up early tomorrow and the film isn't going to finish until 10.30, so no, I can't do it this time."

"Oh, Mum…!"

"How about if you get your friend's mum to bring you back this time and I'll take you there. Next time I'll do the return journey – but you must check with me first before making any arrangements!"

"But, Mum…"

"No, I don't want you to miss out on seeing the film, but I cannot do this tonight. You could always go on another day?"

You have to be calm, and firm. Here's another example, a trickier one. In dealing with your children, you at least have the illusion of the upper hand. When dealing with members of the family older than yourself, it can be more difficult; how often have you experienced the voice at the other end of the line saying: "I thought perhaps I should call to check you were still alive?" simply because you haven't phoned or called in for a few days! Incidentally, I promised myself firmly that I was never, ever going to do this to my own children… and caught myself saying it recently on a call to my eldest son, James. He lives in the same house as us, but like ships in the night, we kept missing each other over a period of about two weeks. I could hear the words coming out of my mouth and could hardly believe I was saying them. There's no hope for any of us, is there!

Calming the terrified monsters within...

I don't like flying. While my logical mind can accept the science of aeronautics, my emotional mind, my heart and my soul, finds it very difficult to accept that several hundred tons of metal, filled with people and baggage, can possibly stay up there.

We all have things that scare us: from the spider running across the wooden floor on tippy toes, to the monster lurking under the bed, the bogeyman in the cupboard. Learning to cope with these fears in a way that enables us to carry on a normal life within the world is an important skill and, I believe, a spiritual one.

In my case, the fear of flying came from an experience when I was 13. My grandparents took me on holiday to the beautiful island of Madeira in the Atlantic Ocean. I had flown before, just a half hour hop to Jersey a few years previously, and I had loved the sensation of flying, so I was looking forward to enjoying a much longer flight. However, as we arrived at Gatwick on the evening of the flight, a thunderstorm was brewing... By the time we took off, it had developed into a really nasty storm: high winds, lashing rain and gale force winds... there was probably lightning as well, but I don't remember.

I do remember the way the plane bucked and shuddered, however; I remember the silence of the passengers and that the cabin staff were firmly buckled into their seats... When we finally stopped on the tarmac in Madeira, there was a sort of collective sigh of relief, followed by a couple of very audible prayers of thanks to God for bringing us safely through. So it was understandable, then, that I should not be looking forward to the journey home... however, I figured that it could not possibly happen twice and focused on enjoying the holiday. We went on a few of the organized excursions while we were there, and one of them took us past the airport – and that's when I got the second shock. The runway is scarily short... with a sheer drop at either end down steep rocky cliffs, into the sea. The pilots have to really put their foot down (or hurl the lever forward!) just to get up enough acceleration to take off – landing is even more tricky, with the brakes being jammed on as soon as all three wheels touch the tarmac! I subsequently discovered that Madeira airport was designated as the third most difficult in the world for both take off and landing. We took off and returned home without incident, something for which I offered up my own prayers of thanks, but within a couple of months there had been two disasters; one plane crashed into the sea on landing, another on take off. There were no survivors on either plane.

So that was it. The thought of boarding another plane filled me with terror and for 26 years I refused to entertain the idea. Then in the late 1990s, my husband Phil was sent to Finland on a work project; he returned full of stories and experiences of how wonderful the country was – and bizarrely, had bumped into a close friend of ours who was living just down the road from the hotel in which he was staying! It took him a couple of years to persuade me to get on a plane and see for myself... I am so glad that he did.

I made a decision that I would not let my fear get in the way of visiting other countries; now I just had to work out a way of preventing it from overwhelming me when the time came.

My first point of call was my doctor; I figured they would have experience of others in the same position and be able to help. The doctor was sort of helpful... he prescribed me some diazepam... which was not quite what I had in mind! To my way of thinking, the diazepam would just be a sticking plaster over the wound, not a solution to the problem itself. I decided to see if

I could find a solution of my own...

I talked to people who understood how planes work; my husband Phil was very patient with me and went through all the physics in language even I could understand! I might have an O Level in Physics, but would not class myself as someone who understood it...

We had a friend who held a pilots' license who offered to take me up in a light aircraft, on the grounds that it would be a kill or cure solution – but the thought of being 'trapped' in something that small almost gave me a heart attack! What if I panicked uncontrollably while we were airborne? There would only be the two of us up there and how on earth would he restrain me and still be able to fly! That was definitely a complete no-no!

Science couldn't help me, I was just too bloody-minded to accept it. It is absolutely no good looking at things in a logical way, if your heart is determined to look at them from an emotional standpoint. That was an important lesson for me: the realization that my way of understanding the world comes mostly from an emotional and spiritual viewpoint.

Once that realization sank in, I felt a lot better. I did not need to burden my mind with all that practical science, because it was not going to make a scrap of difference; my solution lay elsewhere. The main issue now was how to control my emotional responses using a spiritual method and connection.

My life would have no meaning without that connection to the unseen world of spirit. I don't care what other folks think of me on this; it is a case of take it or leave it, this is me. One of the biggest parts of my personal spirituality is a connection to the land, to England. That connection seems to go way, way back, following a line through my ancestors to the earliest times. My research seems to indicate that more and more of us are waking up to that connection; a feeling that we belong here, and have belonged here for a very, very long time. This of course is different for each one of us, and depends on where we feel that sense of belonging lies. We may for example be born in one country, or area of a country, while feeling a deep sense of 'belonging' somewhere entirely different.

I love to read the history and mythology of our country, how we have developed as a people from the earliest times; our traditions, our mysteries, our gods. As I have said before, I do not subscribe to any particular religion, but respect all faiths and creeds. I believe in particular that it is respectful to pay attention to the gods of the places you visit, so I began to research the traditions of Finland in preparation for our trip in the summer of 2001.

A few years prior to our proposed holiday, I had experienced a very profound dream. My dreams tend to be utterly and completely bizarre. Phil is convinced that if I called into one of those dream interpretation radio shows, I would probably be locked up for being completely round the bend!

This particular dream was so powerful that I wrote it down, and illustrated it too – this account comes from my journal. In the dream I was on a journey, with my best friend Tracey, but the journey was not going smoothly. We knew that there was something we had to do, something we had to find, but we could not discover it. Dreams are often like this, but in this one, we both knew it was something profound that could change our lives for the better, some inner truth.

The journey took us through a back alley, the sort of alley you find between the gardens of back-to-back terraced (attached) houses; there were brick walls and high fences either side of us, and the ground underfoot ranged from beaten-down earth and muddy puddles, to uneven cobbles and bricks that had been laid so long ago that they were falling apart and away from one another. There were many garden gates that we could have gone through, but we knew that we needed to find the right gate, the one that took us to where we needed to be. Eventually, we stood in front of a battered wooden gate; it had been painted in a shade of forest green at some point, but the paint had long since faded and was peeling and blistering at the edges of the planks. There was a number 8 on the gate, a number which coincidentally (or not!) is not just the number of our home, but is also our 'lucky' number (as I mentioned earlier). The numerology number for both my name and date of birth is also 8. There was a metal latch on the gate, the sort where you use a thumb to depress and lift the latch. The metal was smooth and worn with the imprint of countless thumbs through the centuries...

Cautiously, we lifted the latch and opened the gate... but there was not a garden inside as we expected; instead there was what appeared to be a small shop! We entered the room and were immediately surrounded by rainbows... small rainbows, large rainbows, shiny, sparkling, glittering rainbows. Some appeared to be hung in clusters, as though they were on silver threads, like a sort of cosmic sun catcher; others were larger, as big as cars, or buses, or football pitches – and no, I don't know how they all fitted in what appeared to be a small corner shop! All of them were moving, shimmering and pulsing with sheer vibrant color.

I was filled with an incredible sense of joy; a joy that made my heart swell and brought tears of emotion to my eyes. I could have stayed there forever, but then a woman appeared... she was tall and slender, dressed all in shimmery silvery green... I knew somehow that her name was Mielikki and that she was inviting us to move on out of the shop and back into the real world. Reluctantly, we left through the front door, followed by some of the smaller rainbows... but they faded the further we walked away...

It is important to know that I had this dream BEFORE Phil even had a sniff of going to Finland, before his company was approached by the Finnish company requiring their services.

It is important to understand this because when I made my decision to research the gods, mythology and traditions of Finland in order to help me devise a method of combating my fear of flying, I had absolutely no idea that historically, in pre-Christian times, one of their major deities was the goddess Mielikki, wife to Tapio, the Lord of the Forests. She is the equivalent of Artemis in Greek mythology, the huntress, the Lady of the Forests and protector of those living there.

When I started reading up on Finnish mythology, the name appeared almost immediately – and rang a bell deep inside the recesses of my psyche. I knew that I knew it from somewhere, but it took me a couple of weeks to remember from where, and when I did recall it, it quite literally made my blood run cold. How on earth could I have known this before? I have always been a fan of mythology; as a child, I would go to my local library and devour everything they had on mythology. But that was mostly Greek and Roman; our village library was only small and did not run to vast archives of the legends, gods and goddesses of other countries – and I certainly did not remember anything relating to Finland or Lapland. I still have all the books I was given on the subject as a child, and a quick reference check revealed that there was nothing even remotely resembling the name or even the country.

It felt like a sign that I was not only meant to go there, but would be looked after by the local gods!

However, I still had to somehow board the plane in order to get there, and the dreaded hour was fast approaching. It occurred to me that perhaps I should work to detach myself from the gods of this land and work on a meditation to hand me over, as it were, to the gods of the receiving country. It's a bit like travelling alone to a new country and being met at the other end by a taxi driver holding up a card with your name on it!

It also seemed wise to begin my meditations before I got anywhere near the airport in order to calm myself and enable my heart to feel in control and at peace.

Each of us has many physical, emotional and spiritual attachments to the place in which we live. I visualize myself at the center of a vast network of threads, some thick, some thin, which attach me to people, places and things.

For example, I have unbreakably strong and shining threads which connect me to my family; these will never be broken. I discuss in a different chapter about how to deal with connections that have outgrown their use, or which you may need to release – even if they are connected to someone that you think you might never be free of. I had a challenging relationship with my father, and needed to loosen the cords that connected us so that I could deal with him at an adult level. It is easy to stay stuck in a childish relationship that gives another person a power over you that you do not want or enjoy.

The cords which I needed to deal with in order to stay calm and collected on my flight were the ones which tied me to England and the gods of England. It doesn't matter whether or not you subscribe to any gods – you will have your own cords, and your own words for your cords. These are mine, so that is what I need to describe.

I bought a CD Walkman (no MP3 players back in 2001!) so that I could use some inspirational music to help me focus. At that time, I found Enigma did the trick for me; since that time I have used everything from Gregorian chant and church music to the wonderful Canto Finlandia CDs and the deeply spiritual music of Yusuf Islam (formerly Cat Stevens).

The preparation work was important, it allowed me to play out the events in my mind before they actually happened; this meant that I already knew what would happen and it would therefore not be a surprise... As I have mentioned before, this technique of visualization is used by millions of people the world over, from athletes preparing for competitive events, to students taking their exams and even folks losing weight! Try visualizing NOT having the bar of chocolate!

The basic exercise to bring me into a meditative state is the same, regardless of what I wish to achieve in the meditation. This exercise is also included in the main chapter on meditation.

Take three deep breaths, in through the nose and out through the mouth...

slowly now, focus on the action of the breath, the air filling your lungs and then being slowly expelled...

Now allow your breathing to return to normal and sit quietly for a few moments.

Imagine that there are roots growing down from your feet, drilling through the layers of the earth, all the way into the molten core. Now, allow some of that glowing core energy to flow upwards, through the roots, up through the layers of rock until they reach the soles of your feet.

The energy will now flow up through your body 'switching on' your chakra energy points as it passes each spinning wheel...

Red light at the base of the spine
Orange light at the navel
Golden yellow light at the solar plexus
Pink and green light at the heart
Blue light at the throat
Violet light at the brow
White light soaring skywards from your crown

In your mind's eye, see your body as if from above, with the chakras energized and glowing in pure color, connected both to the earth and the heavens.

Now, imagine a different strand of light, this one sparkling like an unbearably bright silver firework... it comes down from the heavens and twines around the light energy coming from your crown chakra to form a double helix pattern, just like a DNA strand.

As it descends through your body, through each of your chakra points, the light of each will intensify and become firework-sparkling versions of themselves. Eventually, it will leave your body through the soles of your feet and continue down to the center of the earth.

I think of myself as strung like a bead betwixt heaven and earth at this point; it can be an incredibly profound feeling that fills you with fierce joy, or a cleansing feeling that leaves you feeling as hollow as a reed, and many other feelings depending on what you need right now. Trust in the power of this energy to give you exactly what you need and surrender yourself to it. You won't regret it.

This is my basic exercise; it is not complicated and with a little practice it will come as naturally as breathing. From this point you can take it where you will, but what I needed of course was help to free myself from the limiting fear of flying.

I used the car journey to the airport to fill myself with the energy as described here, and then began to imagine the cords that attached me to the various threads of my life slowly retracting, drawing in.

The threads that held me to the land… visualize them drawing up and out of the ground, coming slowly back to my body like the self-winding mechanism of the electric lead on a vacuum cleaner! This made me feel lighter in some way, as though I was able to allow my mind and soul to float free of the ground and fly off to where I wanted.

Now, I could see the cords attaching me to our home; I don't want to cut them remember, just temporarily bring them in so that they cannot affect my ability to travel, either in body or spirit. Bring them in; watch them unclip from my bed, my bathroom, my kitchen, my garden… Look at the cords attaching me to the kids, to my parents, my grandma; each person appears as a glowing 'ghost' of their physical body. Tell them where I am going and ask them to withdraw temporarily so that I can go without guilt. See those cords come back toward me and into my body. Perform this for any cords that might affect your ability to travel; it will be different for each one of us.

Once I reached the airport, I felt quite serene... until I saw a plane on the tarmac, that was! So I took the diazepam anyway... just to be on the safe side... after all, I didn't know if this would work, or how long it would take to work. Strangely, the diazepam did not feel as though it was affecting me; I was expecting to feel a bit spaced at the very least, but it was a small dose after all. I boarded the plane without incident and sat quite calmly... the engines started and I was fine... we taxied to the runway, and I was fine... then the engines really kicked in so that we could take off and my heart jumped into my throat with a jolt. I love speed, always been a bit of a speed freak, but that brief, hurtling journey to the end of the runway terrified me! However, that was nothing compared to the fear as the plane lifted into the air; all I could see in my head was the plane going up, up, up... and then falling down, down, down! I sat with my eyes tightly shut, gripping my husband's hand on one side and clutching my large obsidian crystal ball with my free hand! I wonder what the security staff thought of this whacking great lump of volcanic glass? I also carried a small piece of flint in the shape of a piece of antler from a local spot I find special; nobody said anything to me!

Once the plane leveled out, I began to feel better; the only snag was I desperately needed the loo – and I was convinced that if I moved, it would upset the delicate balance of the plane and we would plummet (good word that, plummet!) to our certain doom. Of course nothing happened, eventually I had to move and use the toilet and all was well... although the flush scared the lights out of me! I started laughing in the cubicle at the sheer absurdity of it – god knows what the waiting passengers thought outside the door!

Now for the second stage of my exercise. I settled myself back and closed my eyes... I imagined that I was standing with the ancient gods and mythological figures that I associated with Britain... Ceridwen, Bride, Herne, the Green Man, the Cailleach crone – even Robin Hood!

I visualized them handing me over to the gods and mytho-logical figures of Finland, Tapio and Mielikki, Väinämöinen, Lemminkäinen, Aino and Ilmarinen...

In my mind's eye, I saw myself take leave of them with honor and dignity and walk across to the others, greeting them with respect. It's amazing what the power of the mind can do... by the time we came to land, I had absolutely no fear of descending at all – something that has stayed with me from that very first flight.

It does not matter one jot how turbulent and bumpy the descent is, I am cool, calm and collected, where you would think I would be a quivering ball of abject terror! Phil sits there with sick bag at the ready – not through fear, but because he suffers from really bad motion sickness, which affects him particularly in the air, and particularly in small planes!

Now there is one group of supernatural beings I have not yet mentioned in relation to my fear of flying – angels. I firmly believe in angels. There is lots more in this book about how these incredible beings of light can help you in every single area of your life, and as I said earlier, from my point of view they fall into the category of 'cannot possibly do any harm, might conceivably do some good!' (So you might as well believe in them!)

In the days leading to this flight, I was talking to my Guardian Angel almost constantly; he must have been completely fed up with me... but then again, that's what they are there for! If you need help, ask your angels. I say it over and over again, but I'm fairly convinced that most people view me as a (hopefully) harmless crank and don't bother. Why not try it though – you don't need to be 'religious', you don't need any flowery language, or complicated rituals, you just need to talk...

So I'm chatting away with him, as though I am on the phone to my best friend – the only difference is that (for the most part) he doesn't reply. Incidentally, if I am on my own, in the car for example, I do talk out loud; it helps to think he is sat there in the passenger seat next to me. I can confirm that angels always use the seat belts! I tell him all about Phil's job, why we are going, what I am looking forward to, what I'm not looking forward to and asking that he keep us safe and sound while we're on our travels, and look after the family until we return. I also asked for some signs if you please, as it would make me feel a whole lot better if something physical popped up to reassure me, rather than just the ramblings of my bizarre mind.

I got a sign, oh boy did I get a sign. A couple of days before we flew out for that first trip, I was out shopping for supplies for the kids and babysitting grandma. It was a bright day, fluffy white clouds against a background of blue sky, and as I drove back from the supermarket, I was carrying on an internal dialogue (talking to myself in other words) with my Guardian Angel, apologizing for asking for yet another sign…

Without any warning, a seagull swooped perilously close to the windshield of the car, making me jump and slam on the brakes in a reflex action. As I looked up to see what on earth had just almost hit me, I was amazed to see the most incredible cloud right in front of me… looking for all the world like a flying bird… or an angel!

Back then we did not have camera phones so I did not manage to get a shot of it, but I have since seen similar formations and have pictures of those.

The cynical among you will say of course that clouds will form into whatever they darn well want… and you're right – I have lost count of the number of baby elephants I have seen (why elephants?). It's that they form right when you need to see them, right in front of you… and if you are not looking in the right direction, something will force you to see them! The thing with signs is that they come at precisely the right moment. It is absolutely no good asking for a sign and then apparently getting it three days later. It needs to be prompt. Genuine signs touch you in your heart... and are obvious – they don't need tortuous or tenuous links to force you to see them. There is more on signs in the chapter on your angels, guides and guardians.

I cannot ever see a time when I am completely comfortable about flying – but I am a whole lot better than I used to be. Over time, and many flights to and from Finland, I have become used to the sensations of the engines, the turbulence in the air, the floating sensation as you leave the ground for the first time. I always follow my plan; I don't need anything quite as compli-cated these days though! Phil was sent back to Finland in May 2012, to update that original job all those years ago; the difference was that this time, I went with him. When I wrote this section, I was sat in the city library in Turku; two weeks later when I returned home, I was on a plane on my own, something I would not have even contemplated back in 2001. Whatever your fears, you can overcome them, you need to believe that. Practice makes perfect!

One final thing on that original flight... the journey to the airport was not without incident; we were being driven by a friend who was coming with us. He had not exactly finished his washing prior to packing... so as an aid to meditation and a distraction from any forthcoming ordeal, I can recommend arranging and rearranging T-shirts and jeans on the parcel shelf of a car to catch the best of the drying sunlight as you traverse the M25...

Now is all we have, be mindful of that.

I discovered a fantastic book by Eckhart Tolle some years ago; it's called *The Power of Now* and its core message is very simple:

Now, the present moment, is all we have.

Think about that for a minute; now is all you have.

The moment when you read the line has already gone and

you cannot change that.

The moment when you read the next line has not yet happened and you can change that.

So what is the point in lying awake half the night worrying about all the things you cannot change? What you said and he said and she said and they did, or did not do... you cannot change one period, one smile, one frown, one careless word. You cannot change one... tiny... thing. Accepting that is the first stage.

The future has not yet happened.

You can change the future; there are an infinite number of actions you could make, an infinite number of things you could say and it's up to you to decide on what that future will be.

You are probably shouting at the page by now and pointing out, with good reason, that your actions may be influenced by the actions of others, and of course that can happen.

The well-known **Serenity Prayer** explains it better than I can:

God, grant me the serenity to accept the things I cannot change.
The courage to change the things I can.
And wisdom to know the difference.

How many nights have I spent lying in bed worrying about what has happened... which I cannot change... or what to do... which hasn't happened? Hundreds, maybe thousands. I'm only human and will never be an entirely anxiety-free serene being (does such a person exist?), but understanding that now is all we have has helped me immeasurably. Facing up to what is happening, taking positive action, being honest, open-hearted and always acting for good, these things all help me to sleep at night... and on those occasions when I still cannot sleep, well, there is always an audiobook on my iPad!

I am a recent convert to the joy of audiobooks as a positive aid to relaxation. I have found that listening to my favorite authors is a real joy; I take in far more of the story than when I read something for two reasons. Firstly, I cannot skim along and miss bits out, I have to listen to the whole thing; and secondly, I keep falling asleep (which is a part of the plan) and as the iPad is unable to detect at what point I dropped off, I spend the first five minutes of picking it up again, trying to figure out where I got to... I've been stuck on chapter 26 of the current book for almost a fortnight!

This brings me nicely to my next point; being mindful. As life whizzes past at warp factor 9 (*Star Trek* fan to the bone!), we miss so much of what is happening around us. Actively slowing down, so that we experience each moment fully, can not only lead to a calmer existence, but a much happier life.

Think about a special day, your wedding day, a party, a truly memorable special day... how much of it do you really remember? If those special days hurtle past, how on earth can we hope to remember what happened a few days ago!

Here's a simple test: can you remember what you have had for dinner every night for the last two weeks – no, let's make it easier, just the last week.

Now this is me being completely honest, I haven't revised or anything...

Last night (Monday) we had the red Thai beef thing, Sunday... was Father's Day, I made something nice for Phil... what was it... oh help... There was salad, with new potatoes and smoked bacon, and a chicken, red pepper, mozzarella and olive thing (I invent most of my dinners, can you tell?), then Saturday was more chicken salad and on Friday we ate out (easy) and I had sausage and mash (gorgeous) and salted caramel ice cream for pud. Now then, Thursday. Thursday was... erm... not memorable; I've thought about this for ten minutes now and it won't come. Wednesday was quiche and salad, as was Tuesday, and Monday was the chippie as I felt utterly whacked and couldn't be bothered to cook! I still haven't a clue about Thursday though.

Now you try. Tricky, isn't it.

Being mindful, consciously slowing it down, actively experiencing your day and remembering it, can have a beneficial effect on your heart rate and blood pressure and absolutely, definitely helps you feel less stressed...

... What on earth did I have for dinner on Thursday?

Chapter 9

The Inner Voice

In your highest and best interests?

I was stood in a shoe shop in town gazing at the most wonderful pair of boots; knee-length black suede, and somewhere in the ether I could hear a heavenly chorus of angels singing, "Hallelujah!" as they danced around them. They even had the sort of heel I could walk on. Men may not quite understand this concept, but most women have shoes for walking and shoes that look wonderful, but which you cannot walk on. These are reserved for the times when you only have to stagger from the house to the car and then from the car to the event, whatever that might be. They are objects of desire and envy. Young women will try to walk on monstrous heels of course, but once age and sensibility take over, most of us reserve them for non-walking occasions. These boots were not only utterly divine but (sort of) practical too – and I really needed them; not need in the sense of a 'requiring stout footwear' sort of way of course. It was much more desperate than that; I neeeeeeded them! There was only one teeny snag; I was flat broke, and the boots were £89.00.

In my head I was having a very serious conversation with myself; I have no idea how long it went on for (long enough that the shop assistants were beginning to look at me oddly), but it boiled down to this: 'I need those boots, but I'm broke. On the other hand I have a credit card... but that's only for emergencies... This is an emergency, I need those boots... No you don't, yes I do...!' If you tell me you haven't had a similar conversation with yourself at some point, I won't believe you.

We all have a series of inner voices; they are with us every minute of every day, a constant stream of chatter in our heads, giving advice, commenting on people and events around us, sometimes muttering under our breath – or screaming from inside, where nobody else can hear us. It doesn't mean you are even slightly unhinged if you hear voices; it's normal! Most of it is pretty humdrum stuff, but out of all of that internal chatter going on, there is one Inner Voice that you really should be paying attention to, and this is your Inner Voice of Truth. The voice that doesn't care whether your best friend's shoes don't go with that dress, but does care if you are taking on far too much in your life, or ignoring something that is in your highest and best interests, the voice that is a direct line to your Guardian Angel.

This voice truly knows what is good for us; the challenge for all of us is to: a) listen to it; and b) act on it. It is an essential part of spiritual living that you learn to listen to your personal Inner Voice of Truth; whether you take any notice of what it says, or override it, well, that's up to you. Sometimes what that voice is saying doesn't fit with what you think should be done. Or what you think you have to do, or cannot get out of. Sometimes we override what we know to be good sense simply because it doesn't fit with what we *want* to do, even though we know, beyond a shadow of a doubt, that it might cause problems, or even sleepless nights…

Try this quick quiz; I want you to do it twice. On the first go, don't think about the answers, just go with your immediate instincts; on the second, choose the options you would really want to do, need to do, or should do.

1. You have been invited to a party at the last minute by your best mate. She's hoping a particular person will be there, but you've had an insanely busy week and you are completely exhausted. All you want to do is put your (PJs) on and flop in front of the telly! Do you say:

(a) "I'll be 30 minutes; just let me put my face on!"

(b) "I'm really sorry, but I have already made other arrangements."

(c) "I'll come for an hour (praying that this will actually happen), but then I shall have to go."

(d) "Do you mind if I give it a miss? I'm just so tired!"

2. Your boss has told you that you need to stay behind for inventory, but your daughter will be performing in her first nativity play at school; do you say:

(a) "OK, no worries."

(b) "I'm really sorry but I can't do it, it's my daughter's first school nativity play."

(c) "Can I help out at another time?"

(d) "That's going to cause me real problems at home."

3. You love your job, but it is really difficult to get away on time. Your two year old son is with a childminder while you are at work and you find yourself constantly apologizing to your boss, the childminder, your partner and your son. What do you do...?

(a) The job comes first. You need to pay the bills; everyone else will have to get over it.

(b) Your family comes first and your boss will have to get over it!

(c) Tie yourself up in knots emotionally and nearly kill yourself trying to please everyone.

(d) Get snappy with everyone and clean the work surfaces in your kitchen obsessively.

4. Money is really tight, but Christmas is coming, what do you do...?

(a) Bung it all on credit; after all, it's only once a year...

(b) Spend your usual amount on the kids, but tell everyone else you won't be buying for them.

(c) Explain to the kids that this year will be a bit different and tell them why.

(d) Buy (or make) small thoughtful presents for friends and immediate family and set a budget for the kids.

5.   You have a really good friend who has recently split with her partner; she has got into the habit of calling you most nights, usually just when you are eating, or going to bed. You have begun to dread the phone ringing... what do you do...?

(a) Keep on answering, she needs the support.

(b) Turn the phone off and avoid her.

(c) Tell her that calling every night is causing you some headaches.

(d) Talk to her and tell her that you really value her friendship but...

6.   You love your job but it doesn't pay very well; your boss has just loaded you with extra responsibilities, but no extra cash. The new role means it will be even more difficult to get away on time, so do you...

(a) Just do it; maybe they'll pay you extra one day...

(b) Tell your partner that it's a fantastic opportunity and he should be pleased for you!

(c) Tell everyone at work that you will be looking for another job.

(d) Explain to your boss that you are flattered, but no thanks.

7. Your gran is in the hospital, how often do you visit her?

    (a) Every day, after all, nobody else will make the effort will they!
    (b) You started out visiting every day, but you couldn't keep it up, now you're scared to go.
    (c) You have organized a visiting schedule between you and your relatives.
    (d) You really wanted to, but there was no time and now you avoid her as you feel guilty.

8. How do you react when the pressure is on:

    (a) Keep going until you drop, everyone relies on you.
    (b) Eat lots of chocolate and go to bed.
    (c) Do what you can, but make sure you look after yourself first.
    (d) Talk to people to try organizing things to spread the load.

9. You feel absolutely awful; your head is pounding and you're sure you must have a temperature, but your partner is expecting you to pick him up from a night out with the boys. Do you:

    (a) Not tell him you are feeling ill and just do it.
    (b) Tell him you are feeling ill but you will still do it.
    (c) Tell him you are feeling ill and you can't do it.
    (d) Offer to pay for a taxi.

10. You have an incredibly busy life; you work, do the school runs, the shopping, the cooking, the laundry, look after the home and family, organize everyone else and fall exhausted into bed after everyone else. When is your 'me' time?

(a) Ha ha ha ha ha ha ha!

(b) I always have a 20 minute break after dinner when everyone else has to leave me alone.

(c) What's 'Me' time again?

(d) In the bathroom, it's the only private place there is!

How did you get on? There are no 'right' or 'wrong' answers here; it's designed to make you think about the daily decisions you make, and whether you ever put yourself first. Putting yourself first is not a selfish action; it's an essential part of your life.

The first set of answers you selected should show you putting yourself first more often; the second set will probably show you trying to cope with more than you should, or could.

Let's look at one of those questions in a bit more detail to show you what I mean.

You love your job, but it is really difficult to get away on time. Your son is with a childminder while you are at work and you find yourself constantly apologizing to your boss, the childminder, your partner and your son. What do you do...?

(a) The job comes first. You need to pay the bills; everyone else will have to get over it.

(b) Your family comes first and your boss will have to get over it!

(c) Tie yourself up in knots emotionally and nearly kill yourself trying to please everyone.

(d) Get snappy with everyone and clean the work surfaces in your kitchen obsessively.

This was me, in 1995. I was trying to do all of these options, all at the same time! I veered between loving the job because it gave me a feeling of independence and self-worth outside of being a mum – and hating it, because it kept me away from my family! I ended up so physically, mentally and emotionally exhausted that to be honest, I was no use to anyone... I suspect that I am not the only person who cleans obsessively when overtired and stressed. It's a cry for help that screams, 'Look at me! You're all sitting down watching the telly and I'm still working!' However, even if someone comes to your aid, by this time you are more than likely going to push them away because you need to prove to yourself that you can keep going. It a lose–lose situation for everyone and all the solutions require clear calm thinking and taking notice of that nagging little Inner Voice that is saying, 'How long can you keep this up?'

If you do not look after yourself, you are going to find it even more challenging to be there for your friends and family. My Inner Voice of Truth was having its own nervous breakdown trying to get me to do something to break the cycle; in the end, it took a catastrophic incident to convince me that I was probably killing myself. I look upon it as angelic intervention.

We consistently take on more responsibility than is good for us: physically, mentally, emotionally and spiritually. We worry about the people we think we are letting down: partners, parents, children, friends, colleagues, employers, the rest of our families.

How do you start though? If you are the rock on which the whole family stands, how on earth can you turn around and say that first tentative 'no'.

No... Have a practice saying it, go on – "Nnnnnnnnoooooooooo."

That's the word that will help you find more time for yourself, more time to sleep, more time to read, to eat, to exercise, relax... just more time. The bonuses from saying this underrated little word are enormous and varied, but the biggest benefit for me is that I just feel so much better in myself. It can be hard to credit, but doing less can actually help you to feel more confident in yourself. I don't claim to be a psychologist, but I think it's because I have given myself the power to make choices. I no longer feel compelled to do things; I can choose which things I feel I can cope with.

Let me tell you about my life before, during and after my catastrophe.

As I said, back in 1995, life, at least on the surface, was good. I was married to the love of my life (still am!), had two wonderful children, a nice home and a fantastic career. I worked as a personnel and training manager for a national chain of super-markets and loved my job. To everyone looking in, I must have had the perfect life. For me, looking out, I was not having fun. My worst day was Saturday; I had to be at work by 6.30am to do the fire alarm test, I then had to be away by midday at the latest to pick up son No. 1. My manager knew this, but his family was taken care of by his wife; there appeared to be no conflict of interest for him between home and work, so he was more than happy to pile the guilt on me over my leaving work 'early'. Early?! I was contracted to work 39 hours per week, but always did at least 6–10 extra, unpaid hours every week, because I felt I had to show 'commitment'. If I only worked my contracted hours, when all the other (male) managers did extra, how would that look?

Still, most Saturdays I managed to escape… but I knew my manager wasn't happy. If I was late picking up James, well, more guilt piled on. James was 6 back then, and Matt was just 2; we all know that young children are high maintenance, loads of washing, and cooking and tidying up, never ending tidying up. Evenings were spent cooking, washing up, sorting out the kids and collapsing. Days off were spent doing housework, washing, shopping… and yes, I know that this is the life of most mums with young children. I can hear you shouting, "So tell me something I don't know!" But it needs to be recognized that it puts the pressure on. In my case, I piled more guilt on my head because I wasn't seeing my mum and grandma as often as I wanted to, my dad's health was deteriorating and I couldn't support my stepmum as often as I would have liked to – if I did anything 'extra', I still had to do all the rest.

Looking back at it now, from the comfort of a distance of nearly 20 years, I can see that my job was the main issue. The pressure of trying to impress my manager was gradually poisoning my enjoyment of a hard won career. I can remember going in one Saturday, on a beautiful spring morning, exceptionally early, as I was there by 6.00am. My office faced east, with long windows overlooking the busy road, and the sunrise on the harbor. I remember standing still and staring out of the window at the sunrise, 'What on earth am I doing?' I was desperately tired and unhappy… In that moment I sent out a heartfelt plea to the universe to change my life for the better somehow. I didn't know that this was what I was doing; sometimes it's only in retrospect that we can see the pattern, and as I have discussed elsewhere, sending out passionate emotions like this can have completely unexpected results. Less than two weeks later, I had my wish.

The 23rd May 1995 changed my life forever.

I went to work as usual and was called into the manager's office for an urgent meeting with all the departmental heads. We had known that change was in the air, rumors were flying around of a major 'restructuring' within the company and everyone was unsettled; everyone but me. I knew that there would always have to be someone to look after the welfare and training of our 200 staff. It was a bit of a shock, then, to discover that my role was being completely changed. 'Personnel' would become 'Human Resources' (a term I have always hated because it makes us sound less than human), and I would be having a private interview with the manager later. During that private meeting, he went into the detail of the new role; more responsi- bility (of course), less time on staff welfare and – oh god – I would be required to be a key holder. This meant I would also have to be available for alarm call-outs at night, something which was completely impossible for me, as I had two young children and my husband worked away from home most of the time. He then told me that he would not even be putting me forwards for the role; I would be transferred out to a store 15 miles away as a checkout manager. I was in shock; I went through the motions that day, left bang on time and poured out my heart to Phil.

He was brilliant (always is), and suggested that we should go out, for some motorcycle therapy. We would occasionally join the regular crowd who rode out during the summer on Tuesday evenings from Rob Willsher's, a motorcycle dealership near Southampton. I made a quick call to my brother Nick to see if he wanted to come out to play (he did) and collected my grandma to babysit and off we went. We both had motorbikes back then, but I decided to ride pillion on Phil's gorgeous bright yellow 1200cc Triumph Daytona. It was a beautiful evening; we rode with about 40 others from Hamble to Winchester and then across to a pub on the A259 Bognor Road. We stopped there for a while for a drink (nonalcoholic of course) and nibbles, and then Phil and I, and Nick decided to leave early ahead of the pack.

We didn't make it very far; just a few miles up the road. There were resurfacing works on the A27 and the contractors had just finished for the day near the Whyke roundabout; as we slowly approached they had just finished moving the cones to direct us onto a fresh stretch of tarmac. One moment we were riding upright; the next, we were both still sat on the bike, but riding horizontally along the road. I remember eventually separating from the Triumph, rolling over and over and over, until I came to a rest on the verge.

The rest is a bit of a blur; Nick had been behind us, he also came off in the same way. The thinking is that the warm day and cooling evening had caused something incredibly slippery to seep up through the new tarmac, making the surface like oily ice. There were flashing lights, police, an ambulance and we were carted off to the hospital.

Phil got off lightly with a broken thumb, Nick broke his collarbone in two places, I had no major fractures, but my left knee had been the thing sticking out the furthest and it took the full weight of Phil, me and a very large motorcycle as we slid down the road.

I never went back to work.

My injuries meant that I could not stand unaided or bend the leg. It was late August before I could drive, I was on crutches for almost 18 months and ironically, although I could probably have still carried out my original role at work, it would have been impossible for me to stand all day in the role I was being put forward for.

It was a huge shock; going from life at full pelt to… nothing… overnight was far tougher than I could have ever imagined. One thing that you don't realize is how disconnected you become when your focus is entirely on the day to day struggle for survival. For me, the more disconnected I feel, the more the stress seems to pile on, the more anxious I am. I had subconsciously made a decision that there was no point in trying to maintain any kind of an inner life while I was on the treadmill because I didn't have the time to do it – or so I thought. My Inner Voice had been screaming at me to do something about the situation, but I just could not see a way out, and because I thought there was no alternative, I did not even look for anything that might help. There is always something that will help, but you have to look for it and be prepared to make the changes, even though they might cause short-term pain for long-term gain. It takes courage and a clear head, something that having a balanced and healthy energy system will help with. I wasn't accepting the need for change, wasn't looking for anything to help, was stuck in a warped victim mentality. I think that the depth of emotion I felt on that summer morning in my office was enough to start a chain of events that changed my life forever. It doesn't matter by what name you refer to it, Fate,

Cosmic Ordering, a Guardian Angel or an Act of God, something stepped in to save me. The accident may have caused huge challenges to be met, but without it, I would not be writing this.

Recovering took a long time; physically, I still have pain and mobility issues, but I have it under control for the most part and know how far I can push myself. My confidence was really knocked by the long period of being housebound, but I gradually came back to myself over a period of about two years, a time in which I learned to relax again, read, listen to music and play with the children. I also began to draw and paint again, something I had enjoyed at school, but which I had not time for since. I read an article about painting on glass and ceramics and decided to have a go. I discovered that while painting, it was easier to meditate; my hands were busy, I didn't feel 'twitchy' and my mind could wander wherever I wanted. This was how 'Active Meditation' was born and I find it so much easier to focus on the inner life, when the outer life has something else to do!

It wasn't plain sailing of course; a few months after the accident, the company Phil was working for went under. It's something we are all horribly familiar with now, but in 1995, it was less common and came as another blow. I was not earning anything and now Phil was out of work too. For three terrifying months we had no income except state benefits. Thankfully the mortgage was being paid by insurance, or we would probably have lost our home. Two moments stand out clearly from that time: the first is a memory of standing in the local supermarket sorting through a bin of teeny tiny potatoes that were being sold at a pittance as they were so small. I managed to scrape together a few pounds of mud-encrusted spuds which then took me about an hour to peel! The other memory is of agonizing over buying a pair of trainers (shoes again) from a clearance shop. They only cost £6.50, but it was a completely unnecessary purchase – something that was painfully brought home to me after I bought them. They might have had sparkly khaki laces, but they were really uncomfortable and gave me a spectacular collection of blisters! I really should have listened to my Inner Voice.

Your Inner Voice has something to say about every decision you make, but most of those decisions are minor and don't need you to think about them; it's the decisions that perhaps you don't want to have to make, the requests on your time and effort and decisions concerning money that might need attention.

The decision you don't want to make

These are the things that affect us at a deep emotional level, whether to end a relationship, or friendship, how to break bad news to a loved one... Sometimes there is just no way around it, and we have to do it, but have you ever let a bad situation slide and carry on for weeks, months, even years – because the fear of the repercussions of taking action is worse than living with the situation. Ask yourself 'Is this right for me?' and take note of the answer that comes back quickly; that first answer, before you have time to start analyzing, is the truth. The difficulty usually arises from actually taking notice of it.

Can you...? Would you just...?

The most challenging calls on your time are the ones that come from your loved ones. It's really difficult to say no, because you feel that you are somehow letting them down if you do, but unless you learn that tiny word, you may find you feel even worse in the end.

You need, and deserve, your own life. Unless you look after yourself, you won't be able to look after anyone else. You might keep going for a while; the world is full of wonderful caring people who have been supporting their loved ones for days, weeks, months and years, but eventually the pressure will be too much. Love keeps us going for far longer than any other fuel, but even love cannot keep us at our best forever. Everyone needs their own time. I'm not suggesting that you suddenly down tools and disappear into the sunset, or upset folks by announcing that you're not helping anymore, they are on their own now!

Sometimes you just have to learn to let go; you are fantastic at what you do, but there may be others who want to help – they just don't know how to ask you! Learning to ask for help may sometimes go against the grain, but it's not a sign of weakness; by spreading the load you help not just yourself, but those you are helping too.

Encouraging your children to help while they are still very young (and willing) might take more time in the short-term, but will have many benefits, including giving them a sense of responsibility. We are not perfect parents, but we have tried to encourage them to be self-confident and responsible; we have also done everything we can to keep the lines of communication open at all times. You're winning if they talk to you.

Every parent knows that it's a challenge to find time for yourself when the kids are really young, but you owe it to yourself to try. Look for the spaces in the day; there will always be small spaces that you can use to have a cup of tea and relax; however, if you can arrange for someone to take over from you for a while, then you're on to a winner. Even an hour knowing that you are not on call will have benefits; think not just about partners and grandparents, but perhaps child swaps with friends. This is where you offer to go to your friend's home and mind their children, if they come and mind yours for a couple of hours.

Whether you are looking after children or caring for adults, don't be afraid to ask for help when you need it. From asking a relative or friend to hold the fort, to organizing respite care, ask for help. Bottling up stress and fatigue can lead to physical and emotional exhaustion, and as I said before, unless you care for your own needs you cannot possibly be fit to look after someone else. It is not selfish; it's necessary.

When you meet someone new, the Inner Voice will probably be struggling to be heard, especially if you know deep inside that this person is not the right one for you long-term. There's a lot written on the subject of Soul Mates, with all of us hoping that 'The One' will magically manifest out of the mist and carry us off on a white steed. Reality is a bit different; your Soul Mate might not be someone you could live comfortably with – they might not even be a romantic prospect, in this life at least! I think there are different types of Soul Mate, and we might have more than one.

I'd not heard of the theory of Soul Groups until about ten years ago. I was talking to a friend I had met on a Spiritual Healing course and it transpired that we shared a very specific dream, or vision, in which we lived in a Native American village a few hundred years ago. We discussed it at length and our stories matched up in so many details it was spooky! I then discovered that other friends also had experienced something similar leading me to research the phenomenon. I was amazed to see that we weren't alone; there are groups all over the planet with similar stories. The theory goes that people who have shared something in a previous life may come together in this life. Sometimes it's to finish a cycle, or put right something. Sometimes the individuals will realize they are part of a group, but I suspect that more often they don't, and the cycle continues. Soul Mates might be lovers, friends, colleagues, or even enemies in a previous life. If you believe in Karma, it's a small step to see that you might be reincarnated to make amends in this life.

Your Inner Voice and Higher Self knows how you relate to others, knows where you fit in, and knows if the relationship – at whatever level – is one that could be positive and life-affirming, or negative and destructive. Of course we all have free will, and a relationship that may not be in your highest and best interests right now does not have to stay that way. You can change, your partner can change, or you both could change, but it will only happen if you talk to each other. It comes right back to the beginning of this book. The first step in changing your life for the better comes in facing up to the life you have now, and giving heartfelt thanks for all the blessings you have in your life, right now.

It can be much easier to see the truth in someone else. Have you ever been shopping for clothes with a friend who has tried on something that really does not suit them... Have you looked them in the eye and agreed that it looks wonderful when they come out of the changing room with a delighted look in their eyes! It's natural not to want to say anything when you know it's not what they want to hear. If it's you coming out of the changing room dressed in an eye popping outfit which you absolutely love... and your friend is looking utterly flabbergasted, before muttering that it "looks lovely"... how do you react? Can you accept that it's not for you, or do you buy it anyway!

My life is littered with examples of my expert ability to ignore my Inner Voice, but as time moves on and possibilities turn into real events that cannot be changed, so the Inner Voice resets. It's a bit like an internal satnav. When we drive to Winchester, we take the northern cross country route as it's shorter, more direct and much more scenic. If we plot a route on a satnav, it suggests that we go via the A3 south, the M27 west and M3 north, something which adds 15 miles to the journey. However, once we get to the end of the road and turn left instead of right, it resets, figuring out that we have decided to take a different route. Your Inner Voice resets just as fast and, like a satnav, it doesn't judge your actions, just takes them into account and gives you an alternative course. As I have described in another chapter, there is no point in beating yourself up for doing something that later doesn't go the way you wanted or expected it. You cannot change the past, but you can most definitely affect your future.

When I was at school, I wanted to train to be a graphic artist; the careers officer told me there was no such job and I took her word for it, even though my Inner Voice was screaming at me that somebody had to be designing all that 1970s wallpaper! I was disillusioned and left school to start work as a clerical trainee for a huge national company; my dad got me the job because he was a senior manager there. In 1978, you had to fight to do anything different; my options felt very limited. My dad wanted me to be a teacher, I didn't. I had no real idea of what to do if art was not an option so I ignored my Inner Voice and went out to work. I was bored rigid within weeks and even the shiny new social life at the Friday night disco with my friends from work couldn't make up for it. I lasted about eighteen months before being made redundant due to a major engineering strike in 1979. I gave myself a couple of months off, and then, in January 1980, I went out to look for work. The Jobcentre arranged a job as an office junior with a local firm for me, but I just couldn't face it. I didn't turn up on the first morning and decided to find my own job. In the days before the Internet, it was possible to find work just by walking into places and asking if they had any vacancies, so this is what I did. I walked up and down the shops in North End in Portsmouth until I found a job as a shop assistant in a store selling newspapers and magazines, records, cards and gifts. It also sold Pick'n'Mix sweets, something which has always made me smile. At school my friends and I would talk about what we would do in life – and it was mutually agreed that the lowest job in the whole world was selling sweets on the Pick'n'Mix counter in Woolworths! My dad was not happy about my new job; he felt I was throwing my life and education away, but from the first day, I knew I had done the right thing. I really enjoyed talking to people, not being tied to a desk and being a part of a small team in a busy city shop. Within a couple of months I was promoted and within nine months I was the assistant manager with additional responsibility for training any new staff or proce-dures. My dad finally relented and agreed that I was doing alright.

The point here is that although my dad had my best interests at heart – after all, we all want the best for our children – it had to be my decision. Only I knew what would work for me. My children are all grown-up now, and I can really empathize with Dad now; it can be a challenge to stand back and let them make their own life, with all its successes and failures, but it's the right way. I try to follow my mum's example; she has always been there for me, ready with a cup of coffee and some Marmite on toast when life has been tough. Always ready to listen, but not judge. I feel blessed to have such a fantastic relationship with Mum; one of my favorite things is to go out for the day shopping with her, checking out what's new in Marks and Spencer! I can always rely on her to tell me if something doesn't suit me either!

Sometimes you only realize your Inner Voice had been telling you to hold back after it's too late. When I was 19, working in that busy city center shop, I was asked out by a lad who worked in one of the adjoining shops. I cannot even remember his name now (which is probably just as well); he would come in frequently, several times a day, to buy sweets and magazines, and chat to me. We talked about the usual things, music and telly, and I told him I liked musicals. He was nice enough, but really not my type. I should have known better when he asked me out and politely declined, but I said yes, because I didn't have a boyfriend and thought that somebody was better than nobody. Our first date would not have been out of place in a comedy sketch show, as, in an effort to impress me, he had booked tickets for a show at the Kings Theatre in Southsea. Nothing wrong with that you might say, and I'd agree; I had never been to the theatre and yes, I was impressed when he told me where we were going. I was really looking forward to it and reasoned that even if we didn't get on, I would have a night to remember. Oh yes, I had a night to remember alright! The theatre was packed, and I remember the excited buzz among the audience as we took our seats in the center of the dress circle on the opening night of… *Oh! Calcutta!* Now if you have not heard of this particular production, let me enlighten you. It was created by Kenneth Tynan in 1969, and is a show consisting of sketches all centered on sex. Neither of us had ever heard of the show, so you can imagine our complete shock when during the course of the first number, all the performers took off their robes and danced around completely naked! It got worse, the first sketch results in a girl falling into a coma after she is raped, and it then progressed through scenes of sexual repression, songs about sexual preferences, the downside of becoming swingers and even a mind-boggling sketch featuring a man who cannot think of anything to masturbate over! It was excruciatingly embarrassing for two 19 year olds on their first date. I couldn't think of anything to say during the interval; everyone else was chatting excitedly about the 'action' during the first act. Unusually for me, I was silent.

I did see him on one further date, a much safer outing on one of his works social evenings; however, that too didn't go well. It was a Dinner and Disco event on a converted Portsmouth to Gosport Ferry, sailing around the Solent on a summer evening. The dinner, chicken and chips in a basket, was served in a real basket, and the grease from the chicken dripped through onto my new dress of sea green satin. Despite Grandma's best efforts it never came out and I only wore it that once. Worse than that, however, was that in the company of his colleagues, he got a bit drunk and seemed to forget I was there. I knew nobody else on board and ended up sat on my own on the upper deck, calculating exactly how many waves would pass the little ferry during the course of the four hour journey. We didn't go out together again.

I also spectacularly ignored my Inner Voice a few years later when together with some friends we decided to take part in the Gales Trail. This was something organized by the local Gales brewery (now taken over by Fuller's) which involved having to get stamps on a Gales Passport by visiting their pubs. If you completed the passport, having collected 26 stamps from different pubs, you got a commemorative T-shirt. Somebody decided it would be a jolly wheeze to do the whole thing in one night. Back in the 1980s there was no all day opening, pubs opened for the evening around 6.00 or 7.00pm and closed promptly at 11.00pm so it was going to be tight. We sorted out a route and set out at 6.30pm for the pub furthest away from home. I remember this evening very clearly for a couple of reasons. One of these was the amazing proliferation of rainbows everywhere. It had been a beautiful day, but the evening was more unpredictable, with isolated showers dotted over the countryside. As we drove along the twisty country lanes in bright sunshine, at times it seemed that we were surrounded by rainbows; whichever way you looked, there was a cloud pouring rain accompanied by a bright rainbow. There were single, double and even triple rainbows and lots of heavy showers – and yet we were not rained on at all. It was incredibly beautiful.

The other reason for remembering the evening so clearly was not quite so good. The snag with the scheme was that in order to get the stamp on your passport, you had to have a drink. There were five of us in the car and one of the most keen to get the passport completed was our driver, and we all knew that there was no way he was going to drink and drive; he valued his life and license too much. Of the rest of us, two were aiming for passports themselves, one didn't really drink and freely admitted he couldn't hold that much, and then there was me.

I knew I couldn't drink 26 beers, although I did enjoy a pint of real ale (still do). We were all on half pints for the night to speed things along and the idea was that the two of us who weren't big drinkers would get stamps for the driver on those visits when he didn't have a drink himself. Which was most of them. It was a point of pride for me to have a drink in every pub, even though I knew it would not be good for me, so I came up with a way of ensuring that I would survive. I would have a half of beer in every other pub, and a grapefruit juice in every other pub. It did not occur to me that 13 grapefruit juices would hardly settle my stomach, even before adding 6½ pints of Gales finest. By the time we reached pub number 18, I was in agony; 4½ pints of beer and 9 grapefruit juices were wreaking havoc on my digestive system but I was too bloody-minded to admit defeat. By the time we drove triumphantly into the car park of our local, right next door to the brewery, the lads were over the moon with their achievement, and I was groaning on the floor in the back of the car. I'll draw a veil over the next few hours...

It's really difficult to take notice of the Inner Voice when your mates are having a good time and you just want to keep up; we have all been there and I'm not here to judge. I may like the odd beer or glass of something fizzy but I know my limits; and as I get older, I really don't want to spend a couple of days feeling absolutely awful trying to pick myself up again. On the rare occasions when I drink alcohol these days I have a pint glass of water on the go too and drink plenty of water before going to bed, when I wake up during the night and when I get up the following day. One of the benefits of the chemotherapy for me was that it affected my ability to drink alcohol in any quantity and reduced the range of drinks I can tolerate. I didn't see it as a benefit at the time of course; it seemed incredibly unfair!

Sensing Truth

The further we go back in time, the closer we lived to nature; and in order to survive, we had to be able to understand the world around us. Ancient man would have been very much more 'in tune' with nature than we are today. He would have had to understand the weather and seasons, been able to navigate his way around, not just without satnav... but without roads too!

Imagine trying to find your way, on foot, from your home to the nearest supermarket without any roads... just trees, scrub and grasslands... Maybe the odd river to help you out! Just think about it; how would you know which direction to go? For many of us, our inner sense of direction has shrunk away almost to nothingness, and I'm sorry to say this, but that satnav, or map system on your smartphone is just not helping... In a very short space of time, we have moved away from navigating by the sun, moon and stars, to using paper maps, and now, to relying on electronic devices to tell us where we are.

I recently had to travel some distance with a friend. Her only means of navigating was a satnav; we had no idea if it was taking us in the right direction because she had no maps... and when the battery ran flat on the device, we had no idea where we were! I encouraged her to stop at the nearest garage to buy a map...

Meanwhile back in the past, I'm afraid there would have been no supermarket either, so you would have to know where to find food, which berries were safe, where the animals would be for hunting.

Our senses would have been incredibly sharp – they had to be. Our survival depended on us being able to see danger, hear danger, smell, taste, touch and sense danger; danger was everywhere, from the wild animals roaming plentifully across the land, to the weather, finding food, eating food that wouldn't kill us (!), injury and disease and a million other things.

We are wrapped under nice snuggly quilts in our comfy beds at night, safe and secure in the knowledge that there will be food on the table tomorrow. Our worries are very different from those of our forebears and I suspect our senses have shrunk to a mere shadow of what they once were.

I believe that modern life has deprived us of the majority of our intuitive abilities too – but all is not lost! Mother Nature is a hoarder (a bit like my husband) who never throws anything away; just because we haven't needed something for a couple of millennia does not mean it won't come in handy one day, just like the random collection of odd screws in the back of the man drawer. I once threw away a piece of cardboard with a square hole cut into the middle. It had been carefully hoarded for years by my (then) boyfriend and he was not a happy bunny when he discovered it was in the bin. He was also incredibly and annoy-ingly smug when he needed it less than a week later.

You can learn to use your intuitive abilities in the same way as learning to ride a bike. You'll struggle at first, you'll fall off a few times, and there may be periods when you simply lose interest, but be patient; it'll come. There are hundreds of ways to make practical use of your intuition, from deciding on which job to apply for, to which job offer (hopefully) to accept, sensing when someone is telling the truth (a gift most parents would like when asking their offspring if they have done their homework), or when someone is lying.

Intuition can be a combination of using your senses plus that extra spark of knowledge that comes from nowhere; right now, I think it's going to rain soon. I have worked this out from a combination of the skies, which have gone from blue to a uniform light grey, the drop in temperature and the scent of something in the air which says 'rain soon' to me. I could even hazard a guess that it will be heavy drizzle, that penetrating and somehow wetter rain that makes me want to sit indoors and watch the telly with a cup of hot chocolate to hand.

I've used my intuition in some interesting situations; I worked for Portsmouth-based paranormal events company Dark Encounters for a few years as their resident psychic medium. I don't claim to be able to give you messages from your loved ones particularly, although it can happen; my talent lies in picking up the energy of places, and spirit visitors (if there are any) in particular locations. It was a wonderful role, and I was privi-leged to visit some amazing places... in the dark of course. We went to Southsea Castle on many investigations and had all sorts of strange things happening; but one of the most compelling occurred on a Halloween trip. We had lots of people there that night, and I was based in the 'Time Tunnels', a visitor attraction to tell the story of the castle. There are several scenes to look into, each with mannequins dressed in the clothing of the time, posed to act out a particular theme, and each includes the figure of the narrator, a mannequin all dressed in white, with a ghostly white face and hands, poised somewhere within the diorama, ready to be animated and speak to the audience. I found him thoroughly creepy. Anyway, one group of people joined me and we walked around calling out to see if there were any spirits present and learning to use a pendulum dowser. I caught up with a couple of ladies who were staring at the narrator, posed against the back wall of one of the scenes. They didn't like him either, and thought they had seen him move. I explained that he would move when the time tunnels were open, so maybe he had just settled somehow. They weren't convinced. After about 30 minutes, the groups moved on and different people joined me. They asked if anyone had experienced anything so far that night, and of course I told them that the previous group thought that the narrator had moved on this... particular... what the?! He had gone. That did freak me out just a little!

The only time I was ever seriously frightened on an investigation was also in Southsea Castle, this time in the dungeon. I was stood with a lady who was convinced she could see something moving in this particularly dark corner, and I stood with her for a few minutes to see if I could see anything. All of a sudden, there was a sudden and unmistakable movement in the dark and I have to confess that I screamed in shock. However, rather than being a ghost, it turned out to be an estate agent who had wandered off on his own!

If you are sat in the dark, in a place you have been told may be haunted, your senses and Inner Voice are going to be on high alert. Tiny sounds may sound like voices groaning, or children laughing, even the lowest amount of light will seem bright, like the flash of a camera, and you may find yourself feeling panicky for no real reason. It's a good example of how nature can reactivate your senses really fast when you need them; in a supposedly haunted house, you may feel threatened and that fight or flight response will be on a hair trigger – although it'll be mostly flight, as it's tricky to physically tackle a phantom...

Your Inner Voice can also link in with your chakra energies; so looking at the haunted house analogy, if you are in a heightened state of awareness, you may feel a little spaced as the grounding connection of your Base Chakra may not be fully plugged in. The Sacral Chakra survival instinct will be on super sensitive mode. Your Solar Plexus might be overactive, encouraging you to run away – or it might be sluggish, making you feel sleepy. Your Heart Chakra can link to the emotions of spirit people in the location, your Throat Chakra will either encourage you to speak up or clam up, and your Brow and Crown Chakras will hopefully be activated to pick things up yourself! If you don't want to pick things up, you will automatically shut down these chakras; nobody can force you to connect to whatever might be there, which I believe is why some people can live in houses that others cannot tolerate. We are all different; it's one of the joys of the human race!

I should also mention that your Guardian Angel will be watching out for you too, of course.

Back in the real world, learning to recognize what is true and good for you, in your highest and best interests, can be as simple as asking yourself questions such as 'Should I?' or 'Could I?'

The challenge is in acting on the answers!

Chapter 10

Happy

Happiness is a very personal thing.

What makes you feel happy?

What levels of happiness are there for you?

There are everyday levels of happiness; the small things: a bar of chocolate, lying in bed for an extra few minutes, traffic lights in your favor, or a cup of hot chocolate.

Phil makes me very happy, I'm lucky that we have spent a fair amount of our married life actually in each other's company, but if he has to work away from home, we talk every day, and of course these days, we have FaceTime or Skype too. It's a marvelous thing to be able to see someone when you talk to them; it really helps both of us to cope with the separation.

Being with the kids makes me happy; shopping with Holly or Tracey or my mum definitely makes me happy. Reading a good book, sitting on the beach in Padstow, or a late night drink in the Ateljee Bar on the top of the Hotel Torni in Helsinki, with the sun skimming the horizon... that's amazing.

Just as each of us is a unique individual, so each of us generates an infinite number of happiness moments. I have created my own 'Happiness Index' to help me feel good, and I'd like to share that with you.

1. Tiny Moments of Pure Pleasure – the things that give you a warm glow and help you have a good day.
2. The Kindness of Strangers – things that give you hope for humanity. You have a part to play in this!
3. Planned Happiness – holidays, days out, romantic evenings.
4. Inner Joy – the unshakeable knowledge of being connected

to a greater universe.

5. Love – the love that you give and receive, including the greatest love of all.

6. Lasting contentment – a combination of all of the above leading to a feeling of being at peace.

Tiny Moments of Pure Pleasure – I have the Chris Evans Breakfast Show on Radio 2 on as I am typing this, and he has just played *I Just Called To Say I Love You* by Stevie Wonder. As the song finished he read out a text from his wife who had texted to say she was just calling to say she loved her husband. It set off a wave of texts and calls between folks calling to say they loved someone. It's the little things like that which can make your day glowing and beautiful. A tiny moment of pure pleasure. They can lift your spirits and set your heart beating faster, sometimes bring tears to your eyes and always make you smile. These moments probably won't cost a penny but are worth their weight in gold. Try making a list of all the things that make you smile in just one day and you will be truly overwhelmed. This is my list from yesterday:

8.00am Sparkle (one of our cats) has decided to snuggle up against me in bed. 9.20am Phil has brought me a lovely cup of coffee and a kiss. 9.40am Biscuits! 10.30am My runner beans have finally started to grow on the third attempt this year. 10.45am *Boogie Wonderland* on the radio. 11.00am Hang out some washing on the line, warm breeze on my face. 11.10am My order of sparkly beads has arrived! 12.00 Midday Receive letter to say that one of my daughter's final pieces for her Art GCSE is being displayed at an art exhibition in Portsmouth on Sunday! We had no idea she was being considered – we are so proud of her. 1.45pm James just confirmed that he can come to the pub quiz tonight. 2.50pm Phil managed to get all the doors open in the conservatory (they've been stuck since last year). 3.10pm Hit by random moment of joy brought on by sitting in conservatory on a gorgeous summer day doing something I love – writing. 4.30pm Brought in the washing, it smells of sunshine. 5.00pm Phil is preparing all the stuff for dinner so I can finish a chapter. 6.00pm Cooking dinner with Phil is always a moment of pure pleasure. 6.30pm Red Thai Curry with beef created from random ingredients proves a hit with all 6 people! 7.00pm Hug from Holly before leaving for Pub Quiz. 7.40pm One of James' friends from school is in the pub, great to catch up. 7.45pm–11.00pm Loads of fun and chat with our friends Kev and Sue. 11.00pm Shock Horror – we WON! It was a hideously difficult quiz too. 11.05pm Even more shock, we got the 'Killer Question' right to win the cash prize! 11.30pm Celebratory shot of Salmiakki (Finnish licorice spirit). 11.45pm Get into bed and kiss Phil goodnight. 11.53pm Plug in my headphones and settle down to listen to my audio book and drift away…

None of this stuff is remotely earth shattering, but it all builds up into a good day. Acknowledging the good things in your life has a real, measurable, positive effect on your mood, your overall happiness and, in consequence, how content you are with your life long-term. The concept of using affirmations to help you to feel happier is not new; 'Counting Your Blessings' is a proverb that goes right back into the mists of history. You don't need to physically count them by the way; as a child, I thought you had to work out exactly how many you had thanks to a book given to me one Christmas. I also had trouble with 'Advice'. It seemed that every story in that book featured someone either giving or receiving 'A Piece of Advice'. I thought it was a type of cake – let me give you a piece of advice, it's got chocolate sprinkles on!

The Kindness of Strangers – You really do have a part to play in this; if you have been pleasantly surprised by someone who gave way to you at a junction, offered you a seat on the train, held a door open for you or helped you in some way, then you will know the feeling of warmth, happiness and hope for humanity that comes from it. The concept of 'Paying it Forward' is hundreds of years old, but was popularized by Robert A. Heinlein in his book *Between Planets*, published in 1951:

> The banker reached into the folds of his gown, pulled out a single credit note. "But eat first – a full belly steadies the judgement. Do me the honor of accepting this as our welcome to the newcomer." His pride said no; his stomach said YES! Don took it and said, "Uh, thanks! That's awfully kind of you. I'll pay it back, first chance." "Instead, pay it forward to some other brother who needs it."

There are several organizations that work to promote this principle worldwide, but you don't need to be a part of them in order to do your bit for humanity. If you see someone struggling, help them if you can. That's it. Receive a kind action from a stranger and pass it on to another. Your reward is the feeling of happiness.

Planned Happiness – This can actually be a bit of a challenge; you plan the perfect holiday or outing and little things get in the way and build up a feeling of dissatisfaction, so that you don't enjoy it. You need to be prepared for this and pack mood enhancers and, above all, an open heart in your bag. Sometimes things will not go to plan, it happens. Your holiday will be made up of individual days, each featuring those Tiny Moments of Pure Pleasure. Notice them, nurture them, treasure them. The more of these there are, the better the holiday will be – but you will have to work for at least some of them. I'll be blunt: if you sit indoors and moan at the weather, you won't have a good time; if on the other hand you decide to brave the elements and get out there together, you'll have a better time. If you take a pack of cards and teach the kids how to play rummy, you'll not only have a good time, you'll build up a family tradition that could give joy for years to come and be passed down to their kids too. It doesn't have to be rummy of course, but it worked for us! Some people think we're a bit mad going to Padstow year after year, but there is a lot of happiness in seeing familiar faces, playing favorite games and knowing somewhere intimately, noting the changes, bemoaning the loss of the bookshop and celebrating the new restaurants! Everyone looks forward to playing Crazy Golf, from tiny children to grown-ups; our kids have been ultra competitive players, and these days we don't cheat (as much). We barely leave the town these days; when we first started taking our children to Cornwall, we would spend most of the holiday sitting in the car, hurtling along the crowded roads to visit the towns, villages and attractions in this beautiful county. Now, we have a truly relaxing holiday; we park up the car and spend our time walking around to the beach, never crowded even in high summer, trying to keep control of the power kites, sitting in the pubs, reading, shopping, playing cards and of course, playing Crazy Golf. The Crazy Golf is perched on the cliff, it boasts the best view in the town and has a marvelous cafe where you can eat ice cream and watch the world going by in the estuary. What more could we need? We leave Padstow for our traditional visit to Newquay on Saturday morning, a quick visit to Tesco if I really want to cook... and that's about it! I can't wait. It makes me happy just thinking about it.

If your planned happiness is an evening out for a meal with your partner, be prepared to make the effort to be happy! Don't let little irritations spoil your evening – and decide who is driving first, or sort out a lift in advance. Gunwharf Quays is a wonderful combination of shops, restaurants and apartments right on the harbor in Portsmouth; we love it. I had a wonderful 'girly' day with Holly a couple of weeks ago, shopping for prom parapher-nalia; we went there for breakfast and a wander round before going into town. Phil and I then went back in the evening for a romantic meal for two. It was an absolutely perfect summer's day which will shine like a beacon for me in the depths of winter, when the sea is grey and the wind is howling.

If things don't quite go to plan, then dealing with it with good humor and being prepared to turn your mind and your mood around will create a memorable outing that will shine for you. We went to a new restaurant a few years ago; it had been recommended by friends and we were really looking forward to it. I should mention that in my experience, recommending anything always seems to put the kiss of death on it! This was a perfect example. The restaurant was virtually empty – never a good sign – but we took our seats and browsed the menu. Ah. Lots and lots of fishy things which Phil would not eat, and not much else that either of us fancied. The 'British Way' is to stiffen the upper lip and grin and bear it through gritted teeth, but I don't do that anymore! I said to Phil that I wanted to go somewhere else; he was embarrassed about the idea of leaving and would have stayed, not eaten much and not enjoyed himself – and I could not see the point in paying good money NOT to have a good time! I did what any mother would have done in the circumstances: I lied and told the waitress that the babysitter had a problem and we would have to go home! We had a fabulous evening in a different restaurant, and the evening is memorable in a good way, because of what went wrong. We have run away from a few restaurants because of the fish issue; one we were really looking forward to lasted a mere 30 seconds before he spotted the 'Squid Ink Pasta' and ran for the door!

In many ways I think that planned happiness is the most difficult to achieve, because of the level of expectation that has built up while looking forward to it. There are lots of songs that have the answer to this and of course I cannot remember what any of them are right now exactly, but this is the key to it:

It's not about getting what you want, it's about loving what you've got.

If your hotel doesn't quite live up to expectations, don't let it ruin your holiday; get over it and have a good time. If you need to complain, then do it – but don't go on and on about it. Acknowledge, accept – and release.

Inner Joy – If you've managed to read this far, then you will know that I firmly believe that a true Inner Joy can come from that feeling of being connected to the greater universe. Some of those tiny moments will come from this feeling, and some of those tiny moments can turn into quite big ones! Back to my favorite beach in Padstow, and there's nothing quite like a walk along the edge of the sea on a grey stormy day when the wind is grabbing at you, making you gasp for breath. It's brilliant and can bring an exhilarating joy and energy. Nothing 'weirdy', no need for words even. Get out in the wind and try it (God knows we have enough wind!).

As if you had not already guessed that I'm slightly nuts by now, I want to recommend that you find a connection to God in a sports stadium! We are both season ticket holders at Portsmouth 'Pompey' Football Club; we've been up and down a bit in the last few years, with huge disruption to the club as owners came and went and the financial crises swept through like waves on Southsea beach. The thing is that all that chaos behind the scenes did not affect the passion of the fans, the belief in our club; all the madness only made our connection stronger. I'm not suggesting that we treat our clubs as deities by the way… but if you have never been to a football match before, make the effort, just once. When Pompey scores, the roar from the fans raises a vast spiraling energy that connects each of us to each other, and to that indefinable something greater. Despite our troubles (maybe because of them), our spirit has strengthened to the extent that we have treated the last few games of the season in recent years as one big party. We dress up and cheer the opposing team's goals, we sing about our forthcoming tours in lower leagues and treat it with good humor. We will not allow our spirit to be beaten. It's incredible; if I could only figure a way to harness that fierce energy, so that football could power our cities!

We also go to support our favorite ice hockey team, Jokerit, in Helsinki. When they score the stadium lights up with fire and flashing lights, rock music and raucous cheering... When the opposing team score on the other hand, you can almost see the tumbleweed slowly blow across the ice. No music for them.

If tapping into the energy of sports events to raise your connection to God is a bit out there for you, then as I've discussed in previous chapters, tap into your personal places to bring that spiritual energy in to help your happiness levels.

I've left this one until last, because it affected me so deeply. When I first visited Helsinki, back in 2001, we did the usual tourist things and went to see the sights. There are several churches and cathedrals, and I always try to see these, to send out my feelers and see what comes. This is really simple to do by the way; it just means that I sit quietly, or walk around quietly to pick up on the energy of a place. Where churches are concerned, there is a huge variation in how I feel; some feel bright, almost fizzing with Divine energy, whereas others feel desolate and dusty. A church that is regularly used builds up layers of devotion that I believe we can link with to strengthen our connection to God. If you have an open heart and a willingness to link to the spiritual energy of a sacred place, then it will happen, but each of us feels the energy in a different way; I may love one place, but someone else might not feel a thing. If you struggle at first, try sitting quietly with your eyes shut and ask your Guardian Angel to help.

There was one church I visited, on the Isle of Wight, that felt really uncomfortable to me; oppressive and somehow full of fear. It worried me that a church could feel like this and I looked into the history. It turned out that this particular place had been involved in persecuting women perceived to be guilty of witchcraft, hundreds of years previously. Somehow I had tuned into the energy of that time.

Back in Helsinki, we first visited the Lutheran Cathedral; it is a beautiful building, glowing white inside and out, but it feels empty inside to me. The echoing spaces are probably incredibly inspiring when filled with people and voices raised in prayer and song, but when it's empty, it leaves me unmoved.

We then visited the Church in the Rock (in Finnish it's the Temppeliaukio; it was opened in 1969), which is almost hidden up a side street. As you approach, you only see the concrete and glass doorway, no towering architecture, no spires or domes – because this church is underground. It's blasted and excavated from a solid granite outcrop, a circular inner space with rough rock and rubble walls, blast marks scored on the inner rock faces. From outside and above, the roof is a greenish dome, looking for all the world like a spaceship embedded in the rock; from inside the roof is a vast spiral of copper plates. Light comes from windows that undulate in waves between the copper roof and the naked rock. The roof is supported by concrete beams that radiate upwards from the rock, creating segments on the outside of the roof. In winter when the snow is lying on the roof, the light filters through in sparkling and shifting shafts, as the snow slips down through the segments. The altar is placed on an ice age crevice, at the back of an empty space used as a performance area as well as for religious events. The acoustics make it ideal for music events.

I had no idea of any of this as we approached; in fact I was wondering where this church was as I could see absolutely nothing remotely resembling a church! We went in through the doors; I could see a table selling guides and cards and caught glimpses of the internal space through a glass wall. Nothing, however, could have prepared me for the blast of energy that hit me as we walked into the main church. I was struggling to take it in: the unexpectedly large space, the colors in the rock – grey, green, orange, blue, more green... the massive copper spiral roof above me, the light glowing around me. I could feel tears springing to my eyes and was almost pushed over by the incredible energy. I walked around in a daze, I couldn't speak and I didn't want to leave. I have never been affected like that, before or since, by a place – and I doubt whether I ever shall. We try to visit Helsinki every year, and we always go to spend some quality time in the Temppeliaukio; it never fails to move me. The Finns have a rare gift for building sacred spaces; there are many beautiful old wooden churches, including the largest in the world, which can hold 5000 people! There are also some new wooden churches and chapels; we visited the Wooden Art Chapel in Turku in 2012: it's shaped like an upturned boat, the exterior covered in copper plates, the interior all golden wood in a series of arches. It's amazing. Then in January 2013, we decided to explore the strange egg-shaped wooden building in front of the Kamppi shopping mall in Helsinki, and discovered that it was a newly opened Chapel of Silence. What I'm really impressed with is the inventiveness of the new church architecture; it's designed to please the eye as well as inspire the spirit and is a world away from some of our grey concrete churches, built over the last 50 years. I'm pleased to say that this does seem to be changing now though. There are links to all of these churches on my Blog.

Love – You are loved, trust me on this. Even if you feel there is nobody out there for you, there is. Your Guardian Angel, your guides, your loved ones in spirit, they all love you. Your personal happiness will be affected by how loved you feel, and by the love you have for others. Feeling the love of God and the Angels is a constant, no matter what is happening in your personal life; trust in it.

If you give love, you will receive love; pay love forward, send loving thoughts to absent friends. If you feel you haven't found that special someone yet, then it's just that your paths may not have crossed, and you might have to make an effort to get out there and find them. If you are in a loving relationship, then tell them you love them! Now! Often! Don't take your loved ones for granted! Love really does make the world go round, and it has to start with you. George Benson sang about *The Greatest Love of All* back in 1977, a song written by Michael Masser and Linda Creed for the Muhammad Ali biopic. Creed wrote the lyrics while struggling to overcome breast cancer. It's about her feelings on coping with the challenges that one must face in life, about being strong during those challenges no matter what the outcome, and about passing on that strength to our children. Creed eventually succumbed to the disease in April 1986 at the age of 37; at the time her song was an international hit by Whitney Houston. If you are at peace with yourself, if you love yourself, if you can accept yourself for all your faults and little idiosyncrasies, then many other things can fall into place.

Lasting Contentment – Is it possible to be truly content in life? I think so, but you have to combine all of the above to get there. Everyone has challenges to face, big and small, and how you deal with these is key. Going right back to the first chapter, if you face up to what is happening, you will sleep better at night. Am I content? Yes, for the most part. For me, it comes from the love I share with Phil and the kids, from knowing that I have friends and family who love me and from practicing what I preach and not letting things get out of hand or run away with themselves before dealing with them (anymore)!

What do you want from life?

I started this book with the question 'What do we mean by a spiritual life?' and now I am asking 'What do you want from life?' It is a big question, one with an infinite number of answers, and an equally infinite number of variables on the journey...

I want you to think very hard about what you really want and really need from your life. Spend time over it, meditate over it and write it all down. This may be the first things that come into your head, the list of dreams you wanted to achieve that you wrote years ago, or the things that you need from life, such as a home, a job, a partner. You may find that your dreams have changed over time; the things that seemed important at sixteen may have faded into insignificance by the time you reach thirty.

In the aftermath of the cancer, I decided to try and define what I really wanted from life. On a piece of paper, I wrote three headings: Health, Wealth and Happiness, and then sat and stared out of the window into the garden while I thought about it. There was a squirrel out there, running along the back fence; he really was not helping me focus on my task and in the end I gave up and watched as he scampered around the grass and up and down our apple tree. He was very entertaining – and enterprising too, working madly to try to open the bird feeder hanging from the tree to get to the peanuts inside. I had been endeavoring to squirrel-proof this feeder for weeks; he had easily negotiated the plastic tub initially, and taping the base back on had proved useless, as had wiring it shut. I had then bought a wire mesh tube feeder, with wooden base and perches. He had chewed through the perches with ease and knocked the base off in minutes. I could almost hear him chanting 'e-asy, e-asy' at me. This one had a metal base, with wire mesh sides and metal perches. I was quietly confident. I watched for about 15 minutes and then decided to go and make a cup of coffee. A few minutes later, armed with coffee and a couple of chocolate biscuits, I sat down again, and focused on the task… Well, I tried to – the squirrel was now hanging upside down from the tree working away busily trying to pry the bottom off the feeder; it really was very funny, both squirrel and feeder were swinging wildly from side to side, peanuts were flying all over the garden, but the squirrel would not give up in his quest to get the whole lot!

This really was not getting anything done so I turned my attention back to my list. Well, I definitely wanted to be healthy, after the cancer that was a bit of a no-brainer... I wrote this down and then I looked up to see how the squirrel was getting on and saw that it had gone; must have given up I thought... Then to my amazement, I noticed that the bird feeder had gone too! Not just emptied, gone! The whole thing had disappeared...

I ran into the garden to have a look around and see if I could see the bird feeder, but to no avail; he had obviously made off with it to dismantle it at his leisure. We did find it eventually, he brought it back and abandoned it under the blackcurrant bush, the 'squirrel-proof' bottom was missing, as, of course, were the peanuts. (As a footnote, I should mention that the peanuts reappeared, gradually over many months. The little blighter had hidden them in my tubs and pots around the garden, and for a while, it seemed that all I grew were peanuts.) As I went back inside to finish my coffee, it occurred to me that actually, the squirrel had demonstrated some important lessons.

So here is my garden squirrel's guide to life:

1. Look after the essentials in life; make sure you have enough nuts.
2. If there is something you really want, like a large container of nuts, you will need to put in some effort to get it, even if it is right in front of you, conveniently hanging from a tree.
3. Don't give up. Ever. Every step forwards, no matter how small, brings you closer to your dream...

Release Your Inner Squirrel!

You have the tools to change your life. You have the gift of free will; you may feel stuck where you are now, but you could begin to change that right now. Open your heart and mind to a way of thinking and living that says 'I can' and 'I will' and accept that change will only happen when you take action. Each of us has a perfect life in waiting; each of us has the ability to achieve our heart's desire; if we could just but hold that belief.

Accept your responsibilities, accept that the universe alone will not provide... you have to make an effort to make it happen too! Don't give up; every step you take forward, every tiny thing you achieve takes you closer to your dream. If things don't turn out in the way you had planned, then learn from the experience, adapt, change and evolve.

Life is a journey, but we do not make it alone; each of us makes choices every moment of every day that shape our future. If we choose, we can use our sense of connection, our intuitive abilities, to reach out to the universe, to our angels, and experience the incredible help that is available to us; help that is there to enable us to find fulfillment, happiness and prosperity.

Go on then...

What are you waiting for?

Enjoy life, be excited about life; you have an embarrassment of riches in front of you; give heartfelt thanks for every single thing you can and once again... Enjoy your life!

My final words to you come from the Robbie Williams hit single *Strong* from 1998. My journey to try and make something of my life is continuing day by day. I have triumphs and failures, moments when my spirit flies with the angels and other times when I feel desperately afraid. This line, from a song which is about the challenges of trying to measure up to what other people think of you, has become a mantra for me. I had it painted on the wall in the porch above our front door for years! It only went because the porch was demolished, but it still lives in my heart, and I try to live by it.

Life's too short to be afraid, step inside the sun.

Acknowledgements

This is going to sound a bit like an Oscar acceptance speech, and I apologize for that, but there are some people I need to thank. Huge thanks to Jacky Newcomb for her support and friendship; I owe my writing career to your sound advice back in 2005. I also need to thank Mary Bryce at *Chat – It's Fate* for believing in me, and for being a wonderful Editor. I have learned so much from you. I have to thank my best friend and soul sister Tracey, who has been there whenever I have needed her over the last 30 odd years and has been generous in sharing her wisdom and ability to get lost in even the most familiar of places (I share this gift). I was too scared to let her proofread, even though she's better at it than I am, in case she didn't like it.

Finally, I want to thank my amazing and wonderful husband Phil, whose faith in me never wavers. He listens to my most outrageous ideas without batting an eyelid, and somehow puts up with my tyrannical rules over the washing, packing the shopping, unpacking the shopping and then putting it away. Your patience knows no bounds and I love you.

BOOKS

O is a symbol of the world, of oneness and unity. In different cultures it also means the "eye," symbolizing knowledge and insight. We aim to publish books that are accessible, constructive and that challenge accepted opinion, both that of academia and the "moral majority."

Our books are available in all good English language bookstores worldwide. If you don't see the book on the shelves ask the bookstore to order it for you, quoting the ISBN number and title. Alternatively you can order online (all major online retail sites carry our titles) or contact the distributor in the relevant country, listed on the copyright page.

See our website www.o-books.net for a full list of over 500 titles, growing by 100 a year.

And tune in to myspiritradio.com for our book review radio show, hosted by June-Elleni Laine, where you can listen to the authors discussing their books.

MySpiritRadio